An Introduction to Fortran for Scientific Computing

An Introduction to Fortran
for Scientific Computing

James M. Ortega
Department of Computer Science
University of Virginia

SAUNDERS COLLEGE PUBLISHING

Harcourt Brace College Publishers

Fort Worth   Philadelphia   San Diego   New York   Orlando   Austin
San Antonio   Toronto   Montreal   London   Sydney   Tokyo

Text Typeface: Times Roman
Compositor: ETP Services
Acquisitions Editor: Emily Barrosse
Managing Editor: Carol Field
Project Editorial Service: ETP Services
Copy Editor: Jane Loftus
Manager of Art and Design: Carol Bleistine
Associate Art Director: Jennifer Dunn
Cover Designer: Jennifer Dunn
Text Artwork: ETP Services
Director of EDP: Tim Frelick
Production Manager: Joanne M. Cassetti
Marketing Manager: Monica Wilson
Cover Credit: Photonica/Tatsuhiko Shimada

Printed in the United States of America

Ortega: An Introduction to Fortran for Scientific Computing

Library of Congress Cataloging-in-Publication Data
Ortega, James M., 1932-
    An introduction to Fortran for scientific computing/James
Ortega.
      p. cm.
    Includes index.
    ISBN 0-03-003128-1: $20.00
    1. FORTRAN (Computer program language) I. Title.
QA76.73.F25075 1994   93-39563
005.13'3--dc20   CIP

ISBN: 0-03-003128-1

3456 042 987654321

TABLE OF CONTENTS

PREFACE

There are several good Fortran books available, at least half a dozen with copyright dates of 1990 or later. Why still another book?

The existing books have a number of characteristics in common. They are large (500–700 pages), expensive ($40 or more in paperback), and usually treat each aspect of the Fortran language in complete detail before moving on to the next topic. These books also have numerous engineering and science applications, and while they contain numerical methods used in scientific and engineering computation, these are usually given in an abbreviated fashion.

The present book is different in a number of ways. It is short and much less expensive. It covers Fortran in three stages. First, in Chapter 2, the basic constructs of the language are introduced: variables, assignment statements, the IF statement, repetition by DO and WHILE loops, arrays, functions and subroutines, and formatted input/output. In Chapter 2, only the simplest form of these constructs are introduced, but this is sufficient to write rather sophisticated programs.

Chapter 3 returns to the basic constructs for a more detailed discussion, including more general forms and restrictions on their use. By now, the students have enough experience to appreciate these details more than at the beginning of the course. By the end of Chapter 3, most of Fortran 77 that is not obsolete has been covered, and some of the simpler features of Fortran 90 have been indicated in supplements to various sections. Chapter 4 gives a more detailed introduction to Fortran 90, beginning with a review of the features previously mentioned, as well as other natural and simple extensions to Fortran 77. Then the more advanced features of Fortran 90 are introduced: kind parameters, derived types, modules, interface blocks, overloading, and pointers. Finally, this chapter concludes with Fortran 77 features that have already become obsolete, or will be obsolete by virtue of Fortran 90.

This organization makes it easy to use the book if only Fortran 77 is available to the student. In this case, the portions of Fortran 90 can still be studied profitably, even though they cannot be used, but the main portion of the book and the numerical methods require only Fortran 77. On the other hand, if a Fortran 90 compiler is available, simple Fortran 90 constructs can easily be used from the beginning; and the more advanced features rightfully belong at the end of the book, in any case.

The other major difference between this book and others is the reliance on only basic numerical methods as examples, and not example problems from a variety of science and engineering areas. The reason for this decision was threefold. First, our courses, and probably many others across the country, have students from a large number of science and engineering areas and it is difficult to give specific examples that are of interest to such a varied audience. Second, numerical methods are, or should be, of general interest. No matter what the student's area, they sooner or later must perform numerical integrations, solve nonlinear equations and systems of linear equations, and so on. Third, the coverage of these numerical methods nicely complements the calculus and linear algebra that the students are currently studying, or will be studying shortly.

The coverage of numerical methods is necessarily elementary at this level, but I believe it is desirable to stress the importance of errors from the outset. Thus, the three major types of errors—rounding error, discretization error, and convergence error in iterative methods—are given fairly detailed discussions, although they cannot be pursued in any depth.

This book has been used in various earlier forms at the University of Virginia for a first-year course, and I am indebted to a number of students for their comments and suggestions. I am particularly indebted to Mr. Phillip Long, an advanced undergraduate, for his continuing efforts as my assistant, and to Ms. Chris Roberts of the University's Academic Computing Center. In particular, Ms. Roberts' correspondence with Walter Brainerd clarified some important points about the use of pointers in Fortran 90 for which I am grateful to Walter. I also give my thanks to Ms. Brenda Lynch for her expert LaTeXing of the manuscript.

James Ortega
Charlottesville, Virginia

CHAPTER

1

INTRODUCTION

The many computers now installed in this country and abroad are used for a bewildering variety of tasks: accounting and inventory control, airline and other reservation systems, limited translation of natural languages such as Russian to English, monitoring of process control, and on and on. One of the earliest—and still one of the most common—uses of computers was to solve problems in science and engineering. The techniques used to obtain such solutions are part of the general area called *scientific computing*, and the use of these techniques to elicit insight into scientific or engineering problems is called *computational science* (or *computational engineering*).

There is hardly an area of science or engineering that does not use computers. Trajectories for earth satellites and for planetary missions are routinely computed. Engineers use computers to simulate the flow of air about an aircraft or other aerospace vehicle as it passes through the atmosphere, and to verify the structural integrity of aircraft. Such studies are of crucial importance to the aerospace industry in the design of safe, economical aircraft and spacecraft. Modeling new designs on a computer rather than building a series of prototypes can save many millions of dollars. Similar considerations apply to the design of automobiles and many other products, including new computers.

Civil engineers study the structural characteristics of large buildings, dams, and highways. Meteorologists predict tomorrow's weather, as well as make much longer range predictions, including the possible change of the earth's climate. Astronomers and astrophysicists have modeled the evolution of stars, and much of our basic knowledge about such phenomena as red giants and pulsating stars has come from such calculations, coupled with observations. Ecologists and biologists are increasingly using computers to study such diverse areas as population dynamics (including natural predator and prey relationships), the flow of blood in the human body, and the dispersion of pollutants in the oceans and atmosphere.

The common denominator in these diverse areas is that there must always be an algorithm for solving the problem. An *algorithm* is a precise prescription of the calculations that must be made in order to obtain the solution. An example of a simple algorithm for computing the roots (assumed real) of a quadratic equation $ax^2 + bx + c = 0$ by the formula $[-b \pm \sqrt{b^2 - 4ac}]/2a$ is:

1. Compute $u = b^2 - 4ac$

2. Compute $v = \sqrt{u}$

3. Root 1 $= (-b + v)/(2a)$

4. Root 2 $= (-b - v)/(2a)$

Given the numbers a, b, and c defining the quadratic equation, we could—by pencil and paper or by using a calculator—follow the steps of this algorithm to compute the roots. Alternatively, we could instruct a computer to carry out these steps. The main purpose of this book is to set-up algorithms that are typically used to solve scientific and engineering problems, and to see how the algorithms can be implemented in the Fortran language.

Computer Systems

A schematic of a typical computer system is given in Figure 1.1. The center box in this diagram is the computer itself, consisting of the *central processing unit* (CPU) and the *main memory*. The computer may be connected to a number of *peripheral units*, the most common being a *monitor* and *keyboard*, *disk units* with additional memory, a *printer*, and possibly other items, such as a *magnetic tape unit*. These peripheral units are called *input/output* (I/O) devices and allow information to be entered into the main computer and retrieved from it. Also, the whole system may be connected to other systems by a *network*.

Suppose that you are presented with such a computer system, perhaps a personal computer (PC). Without certain *software* it would be virtually impossible to use this system because the computer will respond only to instructions given to it in the form of binary numbers. A *binary number* is a sequence of the digits 0 and 1, for example 10110101101; each computer has an *instruction set* consisting of such binary numbers. These instructions govern the internal operation of the computer as well as the use of its peripheral devices. A *machine language program* for a computer consists of a sequence of binary numbers that instruct the computer to carry out

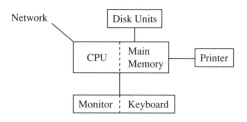

FIGURE 1.1
A computer system

the operations to solve a given problem. In the early days of electronic computers—in the 1940s—this was how computers were used. It was a very tedious and error-prone endeavor.

Operating Systems

One type of *systems software* developed to make using computers easier is the *operating system*. An operating system generally includes commands and facilities for handling input/output, files of data in memory, scheduling, and various other functions. The operating system may be thought of as part of the basic computer system, but it is software, not hardware. By means of operating system instructions, certain basic functions may be handled very simply. For example, the instruction

```
TYPE B:M
```

may cause the contents of a file named M on disk drive B to appear on the monitor. Without an operating system, a sequence of binary machine language instructions would be necessary to accomplish this.

Originally, most computer manufacturers developed operating systems for their own products. By and large, the systems were all different—although some general principles pervaded most of them—and the use of machines from different manufacturers required learning their specific operating systems. Although such vendor-specific operating systems still exist, there has been a strong movement toward general operating systems that can be used on a variety of machines. The two most important examples of this are the UNIX operating system, developed by Bell Laboratories in the early 1970s, and DOS (Disk Operating System), developed for microcomputers by Microsoft, Inc., in the late 1970s.

Over the last decade, UNIX has increasingly become the operating system used in scientific and engineering computation. (It has not yet, however, made much headway in business computing.) But UNIX requires a fairly powerful computer, and DOS has retained its position as the main operating system for personal computers.

Programming Languages

Although operating systems provide basic software support, in order to solve actual problems we must write programs using a *programming language*. There have been literally hundreds of programming languages developed over the years, but most are now only of historical interest. One of the earliest languages was Fortran,[1] developed by IBM in 1957. Although Fortran is 35-years-old, it is still the most used language for scientific and engineering computation. In Fortran, the algorithm described previously for computing the roots of a quadratic equation can be written as

```
U = B *B - 4*A*C
V= SQRT(U)
ROOT1 = (-B + V)/(2*A)
ROOT2 = (-B - V)/(2*A)
```

which is almost self-explanatory (* means multiplication) and mirrors the mathematical algorithm. We assume in this example that the roots are real so that U is non-negative.

Fortran has evolved considerably since its conception. Earlier versions were known as Fortran II (1958), Fortran IV (1962), Fortran 66 and Fortran 77. The latter two were standardized by the American National Standards Institute (ANSI) and implementations of these standards were reasonably compatible on a variety of computers. The latest version is Fortran 90, which includes Fortran 77 as a subset, but has many new features. In this book, we will address both Fortran 77 and Fortran 90.

Although Fortran is the primary language for scientific computing, there are a number of other popular languages used for different purposes. Basic (also True Basic) and Pascal have been used mostly for teaching programming. COBOL, developed about the same time as Fortran, has been the primary language for business data processing. Originally C was developed with UNIX in the early 1970s primarily as a systems language; in particular, the UNIX operating system is written in C. In more recent years, it has been increasingly used for scientific computing, especially for difficult problems. C++ is a newer "object-oriented" extension of C.

Number Systems

The main memory of a computer will hold data, either numbers or characters, and we now begin a discussion as to how this is done. We are

---

[1] Fortran is an acronym for formula translator and it has been customary to write FORTRAN, using all capital letters. However, the Fortran 90 standard uses lower case and we will follow this convention whenever the word Fortran is used.

accustomed to the decimal number system in which integers are written in terms of powers of 10. Thus,

$$2436 = 2 \times 10^3 + 4 \times 10^2 + 3 \times 10^1 + 6 \times 10^0 \qquad (1.1)$$

Here, 10 is the base of the number system, but any other integer $\alpha > 1$ may also be used as a base. The most common choices for α, besides 10, are 2 (the binary system), 8 (the octal system) and 16 (the hexadecimal system). For any choice of α, integers are written as

$$a_p \times \alpha^p + a_{p-1} \times \alpha^{p-1} + \cdots + a_0 \times \alpha^0, \qquad (1.2)$$

where the a_i are integers less than α. The decimal number (1.1) is a special case of (1.2), in which $\alpha = 10$. An example of a binary integer is

$$10110_2 = 1 \times 2^4 + 0 \times 2^3 + 1 \times 2^2 + 1 \times 2^1 + 0 \times 2^0, \qquad (1.3)$$

where the subscript 2 denotes that this is a binary number. Examples of octal and hexadecimal integers are

$$6741_8 = 6 \times 8^3 + 7 \times 8^2 + 4 \times 8 + 1 \times 8^0, \qquad (1.4)$$

and

$$9AF2C_{16} = 9 \times 16^4 + 10 \times 16^3 + 15 \times 16^2 + 2 \times 16 + 12, \qquad (1.5)$$

where, again, the subscript denotes the base of the number system. In (1.5) we have used the usual hexadecimal convention that

$$A = 10, B = 11, C = 12, D = 13, E = 14, F = 15. \qquad (1.6)$$

In the binary system only the digits 0 and 1 are used, in the octal system 0 – 7 are used, but in the hexadecimal system 0 – 15 are used, with the latter six represented by (1.6).

The binary number system is used on almost all computer systems today. The hexadecimal system was used on a few systems in the past, and the octal system is very useful as a shorthand for binary numbers, as we now illustrate. The first eight binary numbers are

$$000 \quad 001 \quad 010 = 2 \quad 011 = 3 \quad 100 = 4 \quad 101 = 5 \quad 110 = 6 \quad 111 = 7 \quad (1.7)$$

By grouping the digits of a binary number in threes and then using (1.7), we may write it immediately as an octal number. For example, the binary number (1.3) may be written as

$$(010)(110) = 2 \times 8 + 6 \times 8^0 = 22_{10}, \qquad (1.8)$$

where the subscript 10 on the last number denotes a decimal number. Another example is

$$010011101111_2 = (010)(011)(101)(111) = 2357_8.$$

In the early days of computing, octal numbers were commonly used as a concise way of writing binary numbers.

Just as

$$0.1468 = 1 \times 10^{-1} + 4 \times 10^{-2} + 6 \times 10^{-3} + 8 \times 10^{-4}$$

in the decimal system, fractions can be written in other number systems in a similar way. Thus, for example, a *binary fraction* is of the form

$$0.101101_2 = 1 \times 2^{-1} + 0 \times 2^{-2} + 1 \times 2^{-3} + 1 \times 2^{-4} + 0 \times 2^{-5} + 1 \times 2^{-6}. \quad (1.9)$$

Binary Numbers in Memory

We next discuss how binary numbers are held in a computer's memory. Memory is usually organized into *bytes*, which consist of eight binary digits (*bits*). Memory sizes are usually given in terms of bytes. A common main-memory size for a small PC is 640,000 bytes (= 640 kilobytes = 640 Kbytes). Larger computers typically have main-memory sizes of several million bytes (= megabytes = Mbytes = MB) and supercomputers may have at least a billion bytes (= gigabytes = Gbytes = GB). The memory size of disk units is generally much larger than that of main memory. Disk memory is also slower to access but more permanent than main memory.

A byte of memory can hold an integer represented by 8 bits so that the largest such binary number is 11111111 or

$$2^7 + 2^6 + 2^5 + 2^4 + 2^3 + 2^2 + 2 + 1 = 2^8 - 1 = 255. \quad (1.10)$$

The first equality in (1.10) is a special case ($\alpha = 2, k = 7$) of the identity

$$(\alpha^k + \alpha^{k-1} + \cdots + \alpha + 1)(\alpha - 1) = \alpha^{k+1} - 1,$$

which is verified by multiplying the factors on the left. Integers of the size given in (1.10) are not large enough for many purposes, and usually 2 bytes are used for integer representation. This allows positive integers up to $2^{16} - 1 = 65,535$. In some cases, even this is not large enough and some computer systems—either automatically or optionally—use 4 bytes, allowing integers up to $2^{32} - 1 \doteq 4.3 \times 10^9$. However, for signed integers, 1 bit is required for the sign so that the maximum magnitude decreases by a factor of 2. For example, with 1 byte only 7 bits are available for the magnitude, so its maximum size is $2^7 - 1 = 127$. (Actually, negative integers are usually represented by the "two's complement," the details of which need not concern us here. With k bits this allows the magnitude of negative integers to be 2^{k-1} rather than $2^{k-1} - 1$.) Table 1.1 summarizes the maximum sizes of signed and unsigned integers for different numbers of bytes (or bits).

TABLE 1.1
Maximum size of signed and unsigned integers

Number of bytes	Nonnegative integers	Signed integers
1 byte = 8 bits	$0 \leq n \leq 2^8 - 1 = 255$	$-2^7 \leq n \leq 2^7 - 1 = 127$
2 bytes = 16 bits	$0 \leq n \leq 2^{16} - 1 = 65,535$	$-2^{15} \leq n \leq 2^{15} - 1 = 32,767$
4 bytes = 32 bits	$0 \leq n \leq 2^{32} - 1 \doteq 4.3 \times 10^9$	$-2^{31} \leq n \leq 2^{31} - 1 \doteq 2.1 \times 10^9$

FIGURE 1.2
Representation of floating point
number

For many computations, integers are not satisfactory and it is necessary to work with numbers using the "scientific notation" illustrated for decimal numbers by 0.4121×10^6. In binary, such numbers are of the form

$$\pm 0.{*}{*}{*}\cdots{*}\times 2^{\pm p}, \tag{1.11}$$

where each asterisk represents a binary digit, 0 or 1, and $\pm p$ is the exponent of 2. The $.{*}\cdots{*}$ portion of (1.11) with m bits represents a binary fraction of the form

$$2^{-1}+{*}\times 2^{-2}+{*}\times 2^{-3}+\cdots+{*}\times 2^{-m}. \tag{1.12}$$

An example of (1.12) is given by (1.9). Usually at least 32 bits (4 bytes) are used to represent *floating point* numbers of the form (1.11). These 32 bits are divided between the exponent and the *fractional part* (the asterisks in (1.11)), which is also called the *mantissa*. Figure 1.2 shows a typical representation in the memory of a floating point number (this may differ slightly on some computers, but the principle remains the same).

The sign bit in Figure 1.2 is 0 if the number is positive and 1 if the number is negative. Eight bits are allotted for a signed exponent, allowing exponents in the range $-128 \le p \le 127$ (see Table 1.1); thus, the magnitudes of floating point numbers are in the range 2^{-128} to 2^{127}. The equivalent decimal range is approximately 10^{-38} to 10^{38}. The 23 bits allotted for the mantissa allow binary fractions of the form given in (1.12) with $m = 23$, and with the mantissa normalized so that its first bit is always 1, as indicated by (1.12). Since $2^{-23} = 1/8388608 \doteq 10^{-7}$, a 23-bit mantissa can represent approximately seven decimal digits. Thus, using binary floating point numbers with a 23-bit mantissa is roughly equivalent to using decimal numbers with seven digits. This *single precision* is enough for many computations, but sometimes more is needed. *Double precision* floating point numbers use 8 bytes (64 bits) for their representation, with at least 48 bits for the mantissa. This allows the equivalent of at least 14 decimal-digit precision in the numbers. (On some computers, single precision numbers may use up to 64 bits, in which case double precision may use up to 128 bits.)

Characters in Memory

In addition to numbers, the memory may hold characters, which are also represented by binary numbers. *Characters* are the letters of the alphabet, (both lower and upper case), punctuation marks, and various other symbols. Usually characters are represented in 1 byte, which allows for 256 different characters (see Table 1.1). There are two common conventions for representing characters: ASCII and EBCDIC. The ASCII (American Standard Code for Information Interchange) convention, which uses only 7 bits, is the more widely used, and we will confine our attention to it. The ASCII representation of the letter A in binary is 1000001, which is 65 in decimal. The complete list of ASCII character representations in both binary and decimal is given in Appendix 1.

Memory and Programs

In order to store numbers and characters in memory and retrieve them later, their locations in memory are specified (much like your street address defines where you live). On many computers each individual byte in memory has an address, but to simplify our discussion we will assume that addresses pertain to each data type. Thus, each floating point number, each integer, and each character in memory will have a unique address, given by a binary number. Likewise, program instructions will be stored in memory, usually in either 2 bytes or 4 bytes for each instruction. (The idea of storing the program itself in memory was one of the most important early developments in computer science.) A sequence of program instructions to add two floating point numbers might be

Opcode	Address 1 (load number at address 1 into adder)	(1.13a)
Opcode	Address 2 (add number at address 2 to adder)	(1.13b)
Opcode	Address 3 (store sum back in memory at address 3)	(1.13c)

Here, each operation code consists of a specific binary number for that operation; in this example, there are three different operations and each has its own code. Each instruction in this example also contains a binary address of an *operand*, the data used by the instruction. Typically (but not always), instructions will be stored sequentially in memory, but the data will usually be more dispersed. However, the address of each memory word containing data will be in the instructions of (1.13a, b, c), which allows the correct data to be retrieved.

The instructions in (1.13a, b, c) are carried out by the Central Processing Unit (CPU) shown in Figure 1.1. The CPU consists of two main parts, the *Control Unit* and the *Arithmetic and Logic Unit* (ALU). The Control Unit decodes the current instruction to see what operation is to be performed, and initiates a *fetch* of the operand from memory (if required). The ALU contains the arithmetic units that do addition, multiplication, etc., as well as units for logical operations to be discussed later. The CPU also contains a small amount of memory, called *registers*, for temporarily holding instructions and data. In fact, on many modern computers arithmetic operations obtain their operands only from registers, which must first be loaded from memory.

Assembly Language and Programming Languages

In the very early days of computing, instructions like those in (1.13) were written out in binary numbers (or octal numbers). Thus, the programmer had to write the binary code for each operation to be performed as well as the binary addresses of all the data in memory. The construction of such *machine language programs* was extremely tedious and error-prone. An important improvement in this process was the development of *assembly language*, in which the instructions in (1.13a, b, c) could be written in a form such as

LOAD A1	(1.14a)
ADD B2	(1.14b)
STO A2	(1.14c)

The *assembler*, the software that converted this program to machine language, would translate the operation symbols ADD, STO, etc., as well as the address symbols, A1, B2, etc., into the correct binary numbers. Although this was a major improvement over writing programs in binary machine language, the programmer had to mirror the machine language code, operation by operation, as well as keep track of all the data.

The next major advance came with the development of *high-level programming languages*, of which Fortran was one of the first. In Fortran, the intent of (1.13) (or (1.14)) could be written in the mathematical form

$$A2 = A1 + B2$$

The programmer no longer must worry about the individual machine operations, or where data is being stored in memory; this is handled automatically by Fortran. In order to accomplish this a very important and fairly complex software system is required: the *compiler*. A compiler translates statements written in a programming language such as Fortran into the machine language code that will actually run on the computer. This is illustrated schematically in Figure 1.3.

The first step of the overall process shown in Figure 1.3 is to write the Fortran statements to carry out the desired computation. Much of this book will address this step, and we only note for now that this process will usually involve typing the Fortran program at a terminal. The key software used at this stage is an *editor*, which is much like a word processor. The editor will allow you to enter statements, correct mistakes, move statements from one position to another, and so on. Some Fortran systems have their own editor; the WATFOR system is an example. In other cases, you may use an editor that is part of the operating system, for example, the vi editor in UNIX or the MS-DOS Editor. Or it may be possible to use a wordprocessor. In any case, you must know the details of the particular system you will be using.

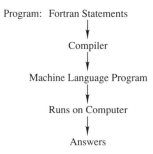

FIGURE 1.3
Stages of a Fortran program

MAIN POINTS OF CHAPTER 1

- An algorithm is a set of precise instructions for solving a problem.

- A computer system consists of the central processing unit (CPU), main memory, and various input/output peripherals, such as a monitor/keyboard, disk units, and printer.

- Operating systems are basic software that help with input/output, scheduling and other functions. UNIX and DOS are two important general operating systems.

- Numbers are held in computer memory in binary form. Two important types of numbers are integers and floating point numbers. Characters are also represented by a binary code.

- Numbers in memory have unique addresses. These addresses are used in machine language instructions, also stored in memory.

- The CPU consists of the Control Unit, which decodes machine language instructions, and the Arithmetic and Logic Unit (ALU), which does arithmetic and logic operations.

- Assembly language programs mirror machine language but use alphanumeric symbols rather then binary numbers. They are difficult to write.

- High-level programming languages, such as Fortran, allow programs to be written in almost mathematical form. Compilers translate such high-level programs to machine language.

- Fortran programs are constructed with the help of an editor, which is similar to a word processor.

EXERCISES

1.1   Give a precise algorithm for computing the sum of the squares of n numbers $a_1, \ldots, a_n$.

1.2   Express the following decimal numbers as binary numbers by writing them in terms of powers of 2.

    (a)   37
    (b)   999
    (c)   1024
    (d)   0.125

1.3   What is the maximum positive decimal integer that can be represented by 5 bits? 7 bits? 9 bits?

2

BASIC FORTRAN CONSTRUCTS

In this chapter, we will discuss some of the fundamental constructs of the Fortran language. In the following chapter, we will return to these constructs for a more detailed treatment, including various extensions and restrictions. The goal of Chapter 2 is to provide enough of the language to allow writing simple, but non-trivial, Fortran programs as soon as possible. In particular, we will write such programs for two important areas of scientific computing: numerical integration and the solution of differential equations.

2.1

COMPUTATION AND ASSIGNMENT

Suppose that we want to compute the volume of a sphere of radius R by the formula

$$V = \tfrac{4}{3}\pi R^3 \tag{2.1.1}$$

A Fortran statement to carry out this computation is

$$V = (4.0 * PI * R * R * R)/3.0 \tag{2.1.2}$$

which mirrors the mathematical formula (2.1.1). As is indicated in (2.1.2), multiplication in Fortran is denoted by $*$ and division by $/$. Addition and subtraction use the usual symbols $+$ and $-$. An alternative way to write

(2.1.2) is

$$V = (4.0 * PI * R ** 3)/3.0 \qquad (2.1.3)$$

where $**$ denotes exponentiation; that is, $R**3$ is the same as $R*R*R$.

The quantity PI in (2.1.2) is an approximation to π and must be defined. For example, if we wish π to be accurate to seven decimal digits, somewhere before the statement (2.1.2) we would have the statement

$$PI = 3.141593 \qquad (2.1.4)$$

An alternative way to set the value of PI is by the statement

$$PARAMETER(PI = 3.141593) \qquad (2.1.5)$$

Assignment

The equal sign in (2.1.2) is the symbol for *assignment*. Given a value of R, and PI defined by (2.1.4) or (2.1.5), the computation of (2.1.2) is carried out and the computed value is assigned to V. R and V are *variables* that correspond to storage locations in memory. Thus, the effect of (2.1.2) is to obtain the current value of R from its storage location, perform the computation of (2.1.2), and put this computed value in the storage location reserved for V.

Variables are denoted by *identifiers*, which consist of up to six characters. For example, instead of R and V we could denote these variables by RAD and VOL or RADIUS and VOLUME. As illustrated by these examples, it is good practice to have variable names correspond, as much as possible, to the mathematical description of the problem. Identifiers can also include numbers; for example, R1 and V1 might be used instead of R and V. However, the first character of an identifier must be a letter, not a number. For example, $1R$ would be an illegal identifier.

The difference between assignment and equality is illustrated more forcefully by the statement

$$V = V+R \qquad (2.1.6)$$

If this were a mathematical equality, it would imply that R=0. However, as a Fortran statement, its interpretation is that the current values of V and R are added, and this sum replaces the value of V in its storage location. Some other programming languages use different symbols, such as := or ←, to denote assignment, so as not to confuse assignment with mathematical equality.

Normally, variables may have different values assigned to them at different points in a program. However, if a variable is assigned a value by a PARAMETER statement, such as (2.1.5), it cannot be changed. This ensures that a constant such as PI can not inadvertently be altered, and also signifies that it is a special variable in the program. The PARAMETER statement will be considered further in Section 3.1.

Variable Types

As discussed in Chapter 1, numbers in a computer can take different forms, for example, integer and floating point. Since these forms may require different amounts of memory, as well as different machine language arithmetic operations, we must declare the variable's type. We do this by *type declaration* statements of the form

```
INTEGER I,J,K                                    (2.1.7a)
REAL R,V                                         (2.1.7b)
```

which should appear before any other program statements. Here, the second declaration defines R and V to be floating point variables; that is, REAL in Fortran signifies the floating point number representation. *Constants* can also be either real or integer. For example, 22.44 and -0.12 are real constants, and 10 is an integer constant. (Note that 10.0 would be a real constant, not an integer.) The variable PI of (2.1.4) or (2.1.5) should also be declared, and we would include it in the declaration (2.1.7b):

```
REAL R, V, PI                                    (2.1.8)
```

In the earliest versions of Fortran there were no explicit declaration statements such as (2.1.7a and b). Variables were typed *implicitly* by the convention that an identifier beginning with I, J, K, L, M, N was integer and an identifier beginning with any other letter was real. Although this convention is still allowed, it is considered very bad practice to use implicit typing. All variables should be *explicitly* declared. Some Fortran 77 systems allow implicit typing to be cancelled by the statement

```
IMPLICIT NONE                                    (2.1.9)
```

which then *forces* all variables to be explicitly declared. This statement should always be used if it is available.

It is common (but not universal) practice to write Fortran statements in capital letters. However, Fortran 77 is case-insensitive: upper and lower case are equivalent (although a few Fortran systems will not accept lowercase letters.) Also, except in a few circumstances that will be mentioned later, blanks are immaterial. For example, I2 is the same identifier as I 2, and INTEGER may be written as IN TEGER. However, it is very bad practice to use blanks in this way.

Fortran 90

Identifiers may be up to 31 characters long and also include an underbar; for example, COUNT_ONE is a possible identifier. Spaces are significant in keywords; for example, IN TEGER is *not* the same as INTEGER. The statement (2.1.9) is part of Fortran 90.

MAIN POINTS OF SECTION 2.1

- Arithmetic expressions use the symbols /, *, +, −, ** for division, multiplication, addition, subtraction and exponentiation.

- Statements such as Z = X + Y assign values of a computation to a variable. Fortran statements of this kind mirror mathematical formulas.

- All variables should be explicitly declared.

- Identifiers consist of up to six letters or numbers, the first one a letter.

- The PARAMETER statement may be used to set the value of a variable that remains constant.

EXERCISES 2.1

2.1.1 Write Fortran statements for the following computations:

(a) $A = \pi R^2$
(b) $S = a^2 + b^2 + c^2$
(c) $w = [(x - y)^2 - (x + y)^{16}]/32.0$

2.1.2 Give declaration statements for all of the variables in Exercise 2.1.1, assuming that those in part (b) are integer and the rest are real.

2.1.3 Indicate which of the following are legal identifiers in Fortran 77 and Fortran 90. Indicate which are illegal, and why.

(a)   FEB29
(b)   29FEB
(c)   FEB?MAR
(d)   FEB_MAR
(e)   FEB93MAR94

2.2

INPUT AND OUTPUT

At this point in our discussion, a Fortran program that computes the volume of a sphere would consist of the statements (2.1.8), (2.1.5), and (2.1.2), in that order. However, we have not yet provided the values of R for which the computation is to be done. We could use another statement to assign a value to R, for example,

```
R = 2.4
```

However, this is very restrictive; we would like the ability to have different values of R, rather than setting a fixed value. For this purpose we will use the *input statement*

```
READ *, R
```
                                                                         (2.2.1)

which allows a value of R to be entered at the keyboard. Then, after the computation of V is complete, if we wish to see what has been computed, the statement

```
PRINT *, V
```
                                                                         (2.2.2)

will display the value of V on the monitor. Thus, by means of (2.2.1) and (2.2.2) we can enter data at the terminal and show the computed results on the monitor. (The significance of the $*$ in (2.2.1) and (2.2.2) will be discussed in Section 2.9.)

When (2.2.1) is executed, the computer will halt until a value for R is entered from the keyboard. In order to indicate that this halt has occurred, it is good practice to precede (2.2.1) by a *prompt* statement of the form

```
PRINT *, 'R = ?'
```
                                                                         (2.2.3)

In (2.2.3), the quotation marks signify that what is enclosed between them is to be written as is, including any blank spaces. Thus, when (2.2.3) is executed, R = ? will appear on the monitor screen. If this statement immediately precedes (2.2.1), the appearance of this message on the screen indicates that now is the time to enter a value of R from the keyboard.

Constructions similar to (2.2.3) are also useful for labeling the results of a computation. For example, instead of (2.2.2), the statement

```
PRINT  *, 'V = ', V
```

will produce a line on the monitor that looks similar to $V = 4.18879$.

A Complete Program

Let us now put together the various statements we have discussed in order to have a complete Fortran program, as shown in Figure 2.2.1. The first statement in this program is the *program name* which signifies that this program is named VOLUME. Although this statement is optional, it is good practice to always start with a program name statement. The second statement is a *comment statement*, as signified by the C (alternatively, * may be used in place of C). A comment statement is ignored by the compiler and is used to give information about the program. Again, this statement is optional, but it is good practice to use comment statements throughout the program to explain what is being done. We have used them liberally in this first program, more so than in normal usage; however, it is better to write too many comment statements than too few. We have used one common convention in Figure 2.2.1 to help readability of the program: Fortran statements are in capital letters and comments in lower case.

The statement following the first two comments in Figure 2.2.1 is (2.1.8), which declares the type of the variables in this program to be REAL. Next follows the definition of PI, and the prompt and read statements. We have added after the READ statement a print of the input R. This is called an *echo* of the input, and it is good practice to include this print to ensure that your input is correct. The computation of V follows, and then the output of V to the monitor screen. The final statement, END, is a necessary statement

```
        PROGRAM VOLUME
C       This program computes the
C          volume of a sphere
C       Declare the floating point variables
        REAL   R, V, PI
C       Set the value of PI
        PARAMETER (PI = 3.1415927)
C       Prompt and then input R
        PRINT*, 'R=?'
        READ*, R
C       Echo the input
        PRINT*, 'R=', R
C       Do the computation
        V = (4.0 * PI * R * R * R/3.0)
C       Output the result
        PRINT*,  'VOLUME =', V
C       The program now stops
        END
```

FIGURE 2.2.1
A Fortran program for computing the volume of a sphere

that tells the compiler that this is the end of the program. An optional STOP statement could also be placed before the END statement, and you may see this in some programs.

Entering and Running the Program

Some Fortran 77 systems allow certain flexibility as to where statements may be placed, but most require rigid rules that are a legacy of the punched cards on which Fortran programs were typed in the early days of computing. These rigid rules are:

- All statements except comments must start in column 7 or later.
- The C (or *) for a comment statement must be in column 1.
- Anything after column 72 will be ignored.
- If a Fortran statement is so long that it must be continued after column 72, a character other than 0 (+ is a good choice) is placed in column 6 to indicate that this line is a continuation of the previous one.
- Columns 1 to 5 are used for *statement numbers* (to be discussed later).

The steps needed to carry out the program in Figure 2.2.1 are:

1. Once you are in the editor environment, type in the program using the above rules.
2. After the program has been entered, execute RUN (or whatever commands your system may require) to compile and execute the program.

Various errors may occur in either the compilation or the execution of the program; these will be discussed shortly. Assuming the program has compiled and run correctly, you will see on your monitor something like

```
R = ?                    (prompt)
1.0                      (entered value)
R = 1.0000               (echo of input)
V = 4.18879              (output value)
```

You have now run your first Fortran program!

We note that some Fortran systems may do the output using "scientific notation" such as $0.418879E+01$ for $4.18879 = 0.418879 \times 10$. This type of notation and output will be discussed in Chapter 3.

Errors

It is quite common to make errors in writing programs. These are generally of three types: syntax errors, run-time errors and logic errors. A

program that has errors is said to have *bugs* and the processing of detecting
and correcting these errors is called *debugging*.

Syntax errors occur when the rules of Fortran are violated. For example, trying to use 1R as a variable name is a syntax error since, as mentioned
previously, 1R is an illegal identifier. Other common errors include leaving
out an opening ' or a closing ' as in (2.2.3), or mistakenly typing R?R,
which is an unknown construction to the compiler, instead of R*R. Syntax
errors are usually the easiest to correct since compilers will detect them and
give back (sometimes rather cryptic) error messages. You may need to refer
to the local system manual for details on the error messages your compiler
produces.

Run-time errors (which include *data dependent* errors) occur after the
program has compiled correctly and execution is attempted. One frequent
source of such errors is unsuitable data. For example, we noted in Chapter
1 that if 32 bits are allowed for floating point numbers, the maximum such
number is about 10^{38}. If we entered a value of R of 10^{15}, then R^3 would
exceed this allowed magnitude; this is called an *overflow*. (If we had entered
$R = 10^{-15}$, R^3 would be less than the smallest allowed number of approximately 10^{-38}; this is called an *underflow*. In this case, most systems will just
set the result to zero and not give a run-time error.) But note that on some
systems integers will not overflow; if a computed integer result is larger than
the number of bits allowed for integers, the result will simply be erroneous.

Another type of error may occur as a result of mistyping a variable
name. For example, suppose you have the variable VARI, but you type it
as VERI. Subsequently, a run-time error may occur because VERI has been
assigned a value intended for VARI. Errors of this sort are precluded by
the IMPLICIT NONE declaration (if it is available on your system), since
the undeclared variable VERI would be detected at compile time. Other
common types of run-time errors are attempts to take the square root of a
negative number or to divide by zero. When a run-time error has occurred,
most systems will print an error message, similar to compiler-error messages,
that will usually indicate the problem.

Logic errors are errors in formulation: the program has correct syntax
and will compile and run without error messages, but it does not accomplish
what is intended. For example, suppose that instead of statement (2.1.2) you
mistakenly type

```
V = (4.0 * PI * R * R)/3.0
```

neglecting the final *R. The program will now compute the volume incorrectly. The compiler cannot help discover this type of error since it doesn't
know what you are trying to do. Logic errors are usually the most difficult
to detect. You must *test* your program on data for which you already know,
or can easily compute, the answer. Only after sufficient testing should you
be confident that your program is correct. We shall return later to this very
important question of correctness and testing of programs, and other types
of errors.

Printer Output

The Fortran program in Figure 2.2.1 displays its output on the monitor screen, but you may want your output in printed form. One way to accomplish this is to put the output in a file that can later be sent to a printer by operating system commands.

A *file* consists of a collection of numbers or alphabetic characters, and is labeled by a *file name*. For example, the Fortran statements

```
OPEN(7, FILE = ' OUT ')                          (2.2.4a)
WRITE(7,*) 'MY OUTPUT IS'                         (2.2.4b)
WRITE(7,*) 'R =', R, 'V = ', V                    (2.2.4c)
```

will set up a file containing the information of (2.2.4b) and (2.2.4c). The statement (2.2.4a) is a declaration that says the use of the number 7 in the following WRITE statements will cause the output to be put in a file named OUT. That is, the statements (2.2.4b, c) put MY OUTPUT IS, R=, V= and the numerical values of R and V in a file that may be referred to later as OUT. The statements in (2.2.4) could be added to the program in Figure 2.2.1 immediately before the END statement. The program will then display output on the monitor, as before, as well as prepare the file OUT for subsequent printing. How the contents of the file OUT will be printed depends on the computer system being used.

The OPEN and WRITE statements will be discussed in more detail later. For now, we will adopt the convention that the PRINT command will be used for writing messages on the monitor, and the WRITE command will be used in conjunction with preparing a file for a printer.

Fortran 90

The form of Fortran 90 programs is much more general than Fortran 77. There is no longer any restriction or where statements may appear (columns 7–72); the code is completely free-form with the following minor restrictions:

- Lines are up to 132 characters long

- A line may have more than one statement, separated by ;

- Statements may be continued by adding an ampersand, &

- Comments may be put anywhere, preceded by !

We illustrate some of the above with the following lines of code

```
X = Y + Z;   W = U + V;   ! two statements
X =     &
   Y + Z                      ! a continued statement
```

Either the Fortran 77 or the Fortran 90 form must be used consistently; they cannot be mixed in the same program.

MAIN POINTS OF SECTION 2.2

- The READ statement allows input from the keyboard, and the PRINT statement displays results on the monitor.

- READ statements should be preceded by PRINT statements as prompts and followed by PRINT statements that echo the input.

- Comment statements should be used liberally.

- Programs should begin with a PROGRAM statement (optional) and terminate with an END statement (necessary).

- Fortran 77 programs usually follow a rigid format.

- A program may contain syntax, run-time or logic errors. A program should be extensively tested to detect any errors.

- Printer output may be prepared by the OPEN and WRITE statements.

EXERCISES 2.2

2.2.1 Type the program of Figure 2.2.1, then run for various values of R. Verify that your results are correct.

2.2.2 Add the statements (2.2.4) to the program and print the results on a printer.

2.2.3 Modify the program of Figure 2.2.1 so as to compute the area of a circle by the formula $A = \pi R^2$.

2.2.4 Write complete programs to carry out the computations of parts (**b**) and (**c**) of Exercise 2.1.1. Declare all variables, input the variables by READ statements preceded by prompts, echo the input, use PRINT and WRITE statements with suitable labels for the output, and use comments liberally.

2.3

DECISIONS: THE IF STATEMENT

One of the most important facets of programming is a program's ability to take different courses of action, depending on input to the program or on current calculated values. Which course of action to take is decided by a *conditional statement*, the most important conditional statement in Fortran

```
IF (A.EQ.0) THEN
   PRINT*, 'ERROR: A =0'
ELSE
   Q = B/A
END IF
```

FIGURE 2.3.1
Program segment for IF statement

being the IF statement. Suppose that a program contains the statement

$$Q = B/A \qquad (2.3.1)$$

In order to ensure that you never divide by zero, you can precede the statement (2.3.1) with a test for zero, as shown in Figure 2.3.1. In general, it is good practice to have a program check its data for any condition that could cause an error before proceeding with a computation.

The program fragment of Figure 2.3.1 implements the logical diagram shown in Figure 2.3.2. Figure 2.3.2 is a very simple example of a *flow chart* for outlining the logical flow of a program. Flow charts will be used throughout this book.

As shown in Figure 2.3.1, the statements PRINT and Q=B/A are indented; this is not necessary, but is considered good practice in order to help readability of the program. The *comparison operator* .EQ. is one of six such operators in Fortran, as summarized in Table 2.3.1. Although some programming languages (including Fortran 90) allow at least some of the usual mathematical symbols for comparison, Fortran 77 requires that they be written as shown in Table 2.3.1.

TABLE 2.3.1

Comparison operators in Fortran

Mathematics	$=$	$\leq$	$\geq$	$<$	$>$	$\neq$
Fortran 77	.EQ.	.LE.	.GE.	.LT.	.GT.	.NE.

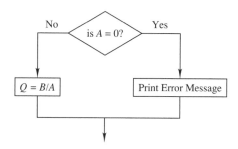

FIGURE 2.3.2
Flow chart corresponding to Figure 2.3.1

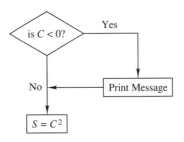

FIGURE 2.3.3
Another flowchart

The flow chart of Figure 2.3.2 indicates a situation in which we wish to do either one thing or another, then continue the program. Another possibility is depicted in Figure 2.3.3, where an additional statement is executed if the tested condition holds. The logic of Figure 2.3.3 can be implemented in Fortran by an IF statement that does not include the ELSE part, as shown in Figure 2.3.4.

The code fragment in Figure 2.3.4 may also be written in the condensed form

```
IF (C.LT.0) PRINT*, 'C LESS THAN 0'
S = C * C
```

This form may be used when only a single statement will be executed if the test is true. If more than one statement is to be executed, the more general construction of Figure 2.3.4 must be used, as illustrated in Figure 2.3.5. In general, an arbitrary number of statements may follow the THEN, and also the ELSE in Figure 2.3.1. This is sometimes called a *block IF* statement since a block of statements will be executed. Note that Figure 2.3.5 also illustrates that an arithmetic expression may be used in the IF statement.

```
IF (C.LT.0) THEN
   PRINT*, 'C LESS THAN 0'
END IF
S = C * C
```

FIGURE 2.3.4
Fortran segment corresponding to Figure 2.3.3

```
IF((A * A).NE.1.0) THEN
   A = A + 1.0
   B = B + 1.0
END IF
```

FIGURE 2.3.5
A block IF statement

Additional forms of the IF statement and more complicated arguments for the test will be discussed in Section 3.2.

Fortran 90

Fortran 90 permits the use of symbols more closely approximating the mathematical comparison symbols. Table 2.3.1 may be modified as in Table 2.3.2 to show the Fortran 90 symbols.

TABLE 2.3.2
Comparison operators in Fortran 90

Mathematics	=	$\leq$	$\geq$	<	>	$\neq$
Fortran 90	==	<=	>=	<	>	/=

MAIN POINTS OF SECTION 2.3

- The IF statement is used for decisions. The basic forms of the IF statement are: IF, IF/THEN/ENDIF and IF/THEN/ELSE/ENDIF.

- The mathematical comparison operators $=$, $\leq$, $\geq$, $<$, $>$, $\neq$ are written in the form .EQ., .LE., .GE., .LT., .GT., .NE.

EXERCISES 2.3

2.3.1 Add to the volume program of Figure 2.2.1 the necessary statements to test if the radius is negative. If so, print a suitable message and bypass the computation of the volume.

2.3.2 Write the Fortran statements to carry out the following flow chart.

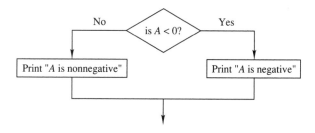

2.3.3 State whether **and why** the following program segments will print R, Z or nothing for the values $R = 10.0$, $Z = 2.0$.

(a)
```
IF ((R * Z) .GE. 2.0) THEN
   PRINT*, R
ELSE
   PRINT*, Z
END IF
```

(b)
```
IF (R .EQ. Z) THEN
   PRINT*, R
END IF
```

(c)
```
IF ((R + Z) .GE. 14.0) PRINT*, R
```

2.4

REPETITION: THE DO AND WHILE STATEMENTS

The volume program of Figure 2.2.1 allows the input of only a single value of R. Once the corresponding volume has been computed and the output accomplished, the program then terminates. If several volumes are to be computed for different values of R, a separate program run is needed for each case. It would be much more efficient if all desired values of R could be entered, and corresponding values of V computed on each run. One way to accomplish this would be to replicate the READ and computational statements of the program. For more than two or three values of R, this would be very tedious. A much better method is by means of the DO statement, which allows repetition of part of a program.

Consider the following task:

For $i = 1, 2, \ldots, n$, compute and print i^2.   (2.4.1)

This can be accomplished by the Fortran fragment shown in Figure 2.4.1, which is called a DO *loop*. It is assumed that the variables in Figure 2.4.1 have previously been declared to be integer and that N has been given some specific value before the loop begins.

The final statement of Figure 2.4.1, the CONTINUE statement, indicates the end of the statements to be repeated. This line has a *statement number*, 10, which must appear in columns 1–5, and it is this statement number that

```
      DO 10 I = 1, N
         I2 = I * I
         PRINT*, 'I SQUARED IS', I2
 10      CONTINUE
```

FIGURE 2.4.1
A DO loop

appears in the first statement, the DO statement. Thus, every statement up to statement 10 is repeated for values of I = 1, 2, ..., N. The statement number may be any positive integer from 1 to 99999.

The CONTINUE statement is nonoperational and, strictly speaking, can be eliminated. Then the statement label 10 would be attached to the last operational statement, the PRINT statement. This, however, is considered to be very poor practice: every DO loop (in Fortran 77) should be terminated by a CONTINUE statement. Also, it is considered good practice to indent the statements within the DO loop, as is done in Figure 2.4.1, and as with the IF statement.

As another example, which combines a DO loop with the IF statement of the previous section, Figure 2.4.2 gives a program to compute values of the discontinuous function

$$f(x) = \begin{cases} x^2, & \text{if } x < 0 \\ x + 2, & \text{if } x \geq 0 \end{cases} \tag{2.4.2}$$

In this program, the number N of function values to be computed is first read, and N determines the number of times the following DO loop is repeated. Within the DO loop, a value of X is first read, the corresponding function value is computed, then the function value, as well as the value X,

```
      PROGRAM DISFUN
C     This program computes N values
C        of a discontinuous function
      REAL X, F
      INTEGER I, N
      PRINT*, 'HOW MANY VALUES OF' THE FUNCTION?'
      READ*, N
      DO 10 I = 1, N
        PRINT*, 'WHAT IS NEXT VALUE OF X?'
        READ*, X
C       Compute the function value
          IF (X.LT.0) THEN
             F = X*X
          ELSE
             F = X + 2.0
          END IF
          PRINT*,'THE F VALUE IS ',F,' FOR X = ',X
10    CONTINUE
      END
```

FIGURE 2.4.2
A program for a discontinuous function

is displayed on the terminal. The output will look like

```
THE F VALUE IS 0.0529000 FOR X = -0.2300000
THE F VALUE IS 7.5300000 FOR X =  5.3000000
```

The WHILE Statement

The DO loop is used to repeat a body of statements a specific number of times. However, if the number of repetitions is not known in advance and depends on the computation being done, then another mechanism is needed. Consider the flow chart in Figure 2.4.3, in which a real variable S decreases by an amount T until S is no longer positive. The flow chart in Figure 2.4.3 may be implemented by the code shown in Figure 2.4.4, in which the statements following the DO WHILE statement are repeated as long as S > 0. This construction may be considered to be a natural extension of the DO loop construct in which the explicit specification of index values is replaced by the WHILE clause.

Whereas a DO loop will only be executed a specified number of times, a WHILE statement can lead to an **infinite loop**, one that will never terminate. For example, it is assumed in the program segment of Figure 2.4.4 that both S and T are positive. However, if T were negative, the statement S=S-T would keep increasing S; thus, S would always be positive and the loop would never terminate. (Actually, in floating point arithmetic, if T were very large, eventually overflow would occur and the loop would terminate with a run-time error. However, if the magnitude of T is not

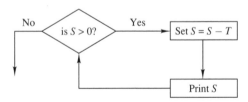

FIGURE 2.4.3
A flow chart

```
DO WHILE (S.GT.0)
    S = S - T
    PRINT*, S
END DO
```

FIGURE 2.4.4
A WHILE loop

large, eventually the computed value of S+T would equal S, and thereafter S would not change.)

Another caveat about the DO WHILE statement is that it is *not* part of the Fortran 77 standard. However, many Fortran 77 compilers either implement it or the following variation:

```
WHILE (S.GT.0) DO
   S = S - T
   PRINT*, S
END WHILE
```

Next we give another example of the use of the WHILE statement. The infinite series for the exponential is

$$e^x = \sum_{k=0}^{\infty} \frac{x^k}{k!} = 1 + x + \frac{x^2}{2} + \cdots + \frac{x^n}{n!} + \cdots$$

Suppose that we wish to approximate e^x by computing the partial sums[1]

$$E_n = 1 + x + \frac{x^2}{2} + \cdots + \frac{x^n}{n!} \tag{2.4.3}$$

How do we know how many terms to take? One criterion is to keep adding the terms of the series until the last added is suitably small:

$$\frac{|x^n|}{n!} \leq \varepsilon \tag{2.4.4}$$

where ε is a given small parameter (for example, $\varepsilon = 10^{-5}$). Thus, n in (2.4.3) is the smallest value for which (2.4.4) holds. Figure 2.4.5 gives a Fortran program for computing the approximation (2.4.3).

In the program of Figure 2.4.5, X and EPS are first read in and printed. (Note that there must be a space between the values of X and EPS when you type them at the keyboard.) E is the current approximation to e^x, initialized as 1.0, and DE is the next term of the series, also initialized as 1.0. Thus, the first time through the WHILE loop, DE = (X*1.0)/1.0=X, which is added to E=1.0. The next time through the loop DE = (X*X)/2.0 = X**2/2, and so on. In the WHILE statement test, ABS(DE) is the absolute value of the current value of DE; thus, we repeat the statements in the WHILE loop until (2.4.4) is satisfied. Each time through the WHILE loop we print the current approximation E, the number of terms in the series so far, N, and the last term added to the series, DE. In Figure 2.4.6 we give sample output for X=1 with $\varepsilon = 0.0001$. As expected, the successive approximations in Figure 2.4.6 give better and better approximations to $e = 2.718282$.

---

[1]We note that this is not the best way to approximate e^x. It is given only to illustrate approximation of an infinite series.

```
        PROGRAM EXPON
C This program approximates an exponential
C    by a truncated series
        REAL E, DE, N, EPS, X
        PRINT*, 'WHAT IS X? WHAT IS EPS?'
        READ*, X, EPS
        PRINT*, 'X = ', X, 'EPS = ', EPS
C Initialize E, DE, N
        E = 1.0
        DE = 1.0
        N = 1.0
C Compute the series until last term is
C    less than or equal to EPS
        DO WHILE (ABS(DE).GT.EPS)
           DE = (X*DE)/N
           E = E + DE
           N = N + 1.0
           PRINT*, 'E = ',E,'N = ',N,'DE = ',DE
        END DO
        END
```

FIGURE 2.4.5
A program for approximating the exponential

```
X = 1.000000    EPS = 0.0001000
E = 2.000000    N = 2.000000   DE = 1.000000
E = 2.500000    N = 3.000000   DE = 0.500000
E = 2.666667    N = 4.000000   DE = 0.166667
E = 2.708333    N = 5.000000   DE = 0.041667
E = 2.716667    N = 6.000000   DE = 0.008333
E = 2.718056    N = 7.000000   DE = 0.001389
E = 2.718254    N = 8.000000   DE = 0.000198
E = 2.718279    N = 9.000000   DE = 0.000025
```

FIGURE 2.4.6
Output of exponential program of Figure 2.4.5

The GO TO Statement

In the event that neither the WHILE DO nor DO WHILE construction is available, the flow chart of Figure 2.4.3 may be implemented using a GO TO statement. In general, Fortran statements are executed sequentially, in the order in which they are written. The GO TO statement breaks this sequential flow by transferring to another statement, as illustrated in Figure 2.4.7. In particular, the GO TO statement in Figure 2.4.7(a) performs a transfer to the statement labeled 20, the IF statement. The effect is that the

```
20 IF(S.GT.0) THEN        20 CONTINUE
      S = S - T               S = S - T
      PRINT*, S               PRINT*, S
      GO TO 20                IF(S.GT.0) GO TO 20
   END IF
```

(a) Pre-test   (b) Post-test

FIGURE 2.4.7
A loop using GO TO

loop will continue executing as long as $S > 0$. In general, GO TO *statement number* will execute a transfer to the statement with the given statement number.

Figure 2.4.7 illustrates two different ways of implementing the loop of Figure 2.4.3 with a GO TO statement. The first, Figure 2.4.7(*a*), is a "pre-test" loop in which the test is performed in the first statement of the loop; this mirrors the DO WHILE loop of Figure 2.4.4. The second way is a "post-test" loop, in which the test is the last statement of the loop. The two loops in Figure 2.4.7 are equivalent provided that $S > 0$ initially. If, however, $S \le 0$, the loop in Figure 2.4.7(*b*) is still executed once.

The GO TO statement has long been considered dangerous and should be avoided, especially when there are reasonable alternatives. However, the GO TO statement in the short loops in Figure 2.4.7 is rather innocuous. The real danger of the GO TO statement is a transfer to a distant statement, perhaps several hundred lines of code away, which makes the program more difficult to understand.

Sentinels

Another common way to terminate loops is to use a special number, (or character) called a *sentinel*. Suppose that in the context of the volume program of Figure 2.2.1, we wish to keep reading in radii (R) and computing volumes, (V), an arbitrary number of times, until R=-1.0 is read. This special value of R is the sentinel. We can implement this by the code shown in Figure 2.4.8.

```
READ*, R
DO WHILE(R.NE.-1.0)
    V = (4.0 * PI * R ** 3)/3.0
    PRINT*, R, V
    READ *, R
END DO
```

FIGURE 2.4.8
Termination by a sentinel

Alternatively, rather than testing for a specific value of R we could test for any negative value. Then the test in the WHILE statement would be changed to R.GE.0. (See Exercise 2.4.7).

Fortran 90

In Fortran 90, the DO loop may be written in the form

```
DO I = 1,N
```

Statements

```
END DO
```

without a CONTINUE statement or a statement label; in this example, all statements between DO and END DO are repeated N times. (This form of the DO statement is also available in some Fortran 77 systems, such as WATFOR.) The DO WHILE construction (but not the WHILE DO) is part of Fortran 90. An alternative to the DO WHILE statement is the following construction:

```
DO
```

Statements

```
IF (X.LE.10) EXIT
END DO
```

in which the DO loop has no index or test at all. If the argument of the IF statement is true, the DO loop will be terminated and control passed to the statement following END DO. The IF statement need not be the statement before END DO and may be placed anywhere between DO and END DO. However, clarity is enhanced if EXIT is in either the first or last statement within the DO body.

MAIN POINTS OF SECTION 2.4

- A given number of repetitions may be effected by a DO loop.
- An indeterminate number of repititions may be effected by a WHILE loop, if this feature is available in your Fortran 77 system.
- Transfer of program control may be achieved by the GO TO statement, but this statement should be used only if necessary.
- Sentinels are special values of a variable used to terminate a loop.

EXERCISES 2.4

2.4.1 Modify the volume program of Figure 2.2.1 to read a value N at the outset, and compute and output N values of the volume. Be sure all variables are properly declared. Include a prompt for the read of N, and then an echo of its value. Move the WRITE statement so that 'MY OUTPUT IS' prints only once.

2.4.2 Write a program segment that adds B to A 20 times and prints all the sums.

2.4.3 Write a program segment that will add B to A until the sum exceeds 100.

2.4.4 What are the values of R and S at the conclusion of each of the following loops, if R=20.0 and S=2.0 when the loop begins?

(a)
```
        DO 10 I = 1, 5
          R = R + S
          S = S * S
     10 CONTINUE
```

(b)
```
        DO WHILE (S.LE.100)
          R = R + S
          S = S * S
        END DO
```

2.4.5 Run the program of Figure 2.4.2 for several values of X, both positive and negative. Verify that the computed results are correct.

2.4.6 The series for $\cos(x)$ is

$$\cos(x) = 1 - \frac{x^2}{2} + \frac{x^4}{4!} + \cdots + \frac{(-1)^n x^{2n}}{(2n)!} + \cdots$$

Write a Fortran program similar to that of Figure 2.4.5 to approximate $\cos(x)$ by k terms of this series. Check your program for various values of x for which you know the value of $\cos(x)$. (For example, $\cos(\frac{\pi}{4}) = \frac{\sqrt{2}}{2}$.)

2.4.7 Modify the program of Figure 2.4.8 so that it will terminate whenever a negative value of R is read.

2.5

SUBPROGRAMS

In many problems it is necessary to compute a given function in different parts of the program (but, perhaps, with different arguments). It would be tedious to write the Fortran statements for the same function over and over each time it was used. Fortran and other programming languages allow a function to be defined once and for all, and then it can be *called* whenever it is needed. More generally, any program segment that is to be used repeatedly may be defined as a separate *subroutine* that may be called when needed. Such functions and subroutines are *subprograms* (or *procedures* in Fortran 90). Subprograms also allow a large program to be broken up into smaller parts that may be tested separately. This aspect of subprograms will be discussed after we consider their basic forms.

Intrinsic Functions

For most elementary mathematical functions encountered in calculus, function subprograms have already been written and are included as part of Fortran. These functions are called *intrinsic*. For example, suppose that we wish to compute $\sqrt{x}$. This may be achieved in Fortran by the statement

$$Y = SQRT (X) \tag{2.5.1}$$

which sets Y equal to the square root of X (X must be nonnegative or a run-time error will occur). A sample of these functions is given in Table 2.5.1 and a complete list is given in Appendix 2. We already used the ABS intrinsic function in the program of Figure 2.4.5.

As a second example of the use of the intrinsic functions in Table 2.5.1, the Fortran statement

$$Z = SIN(X) + EXP(ABS(X))$$

will compute $\sin(x) + e^{|x|}$. Note that in this example the argument of EXP is the function value ABS (X). In general, the argument of a function may be any arithmetic expression.

Declared Functions

In addition to the intrinsic functions that are part of Fortran, functions may also be defined by the programmer. Figure 2.5.1 gives an example of a function program to compute the discontinuous function

$$f(x) = \begin{cases} x^2, & \text{if } x < 0 \\ x + 2, & \text{if } x \geq 0 \end{cases} \tag{2.5.2}$$

used in the program of Figure 2.4.2.

TABLE 2.5.1

Some Fortran intrinsic functions

Mathematical	$\sqrt{x}$	$\sin(x)$	e^x	$|x|$
Fortran	SQRT (X)	SIN (X)	EXP (X)	ABS (X)

```
REAL FUNCTION F(X)
   REAL X
   IF (X. LT. 0) THEN
      F = X * X
   ELSE
      F = X + 2.0
   END IF
END
```

FIGURE 2.5.1
A Fortran function

The first statement of Figure 2.5.1 declares F to be a function of type REAL, so that values of F(X) will be floating point numbers, and the second statement declares the *argument* X to be of type REAL. Alternatively, if X took on only integer values, and was declared as integer, F could have been declared to be integer also by the statement

```
INTEGER FUNCTION F(X)
```

In either case, since F takes on numerical values, it is necessary to define its type, just as if it were a variable. A declaration of the type of the function, by a statement of the form REAL F, should also appear in the program that uses the function.

The IF statement in Figure 2.5.1 is the same as that used in Figure 2.4.2. An important point is that a value is assigned to F by one of the two possible assignment statements. In general, somewhere in the body of a function program a value must be assigned to the function name. The END statement indicates that the function definition is complete. (An optional RETURN statement may precede the END statement; this may be seen in older Fortran programs.)

Once the function has been defined it may be used in the same way as an intrinsic function. For example, the following statements may appear in different parts of the main program.

$$Y = F(4.0) \tag{2.5.3a}$$
$$PRINT*, \ F(W) \tag{2.5.3b}$$
$$Y = F(3.0*W) + Z \tag{2.5.3c}$$

Note that in all three cases in (2.5.3) the argument of the function is not X, as it is in the definition of the function in Figure 2.5.1. The variable X in Figure 2.5.1 is a *dummy variable* or *formal argument* whose actual value will be supplied when the function is *invoked* or *called*, as is being done in (2.5.3). The function name, however, must always appear exactly as it does in the definition. Thus, F is in all three statements of (2.5.3). The first statement, (2.5.3a), will set Y=6.0. If W is −2.0, (2.5.3b) will print 4.0, and if Z is 4.0, (2.5.3c) will set Y to equal $36.0 + 4.0 = 40.0$. The statement (2.5.3c) illustrates that arithmetic expressions, not just single variables, may be used as arguments when the function is called.

A function such as that of Figure 2.5.1 is defined outside the main program. This is illustrated in Figure 2.5.2, which is the program of Figure 2.4.2 rewritten to use the function of Figure 2.5.1.

Statement Functions

If a function is sufficiently simple that it may be expressed by a single assignment statement, then the function may be defined in Fortran as a *statement function*. For example, the function

$$f(x) = x^3 + 2x^2$$

may be defined as illustrated in Figure 2.5.3.

In Figure 2.5.3, the function F is *defined* by the assignment statement. This statement must appear in the main program before any executable statements, but after any declaration statements. Note that F is declared to

```
      PROGRAM DISFUN
C This program computes N values of a
C    discontinuous function
      REAL X, F
      INTEGER I, N
      PRINT*, 'HOW MANY VALUES OF THE FUNCTION?'
      READ*, N
      DO 10 I = 1, N
         PRINT*, 'WHAT IS THE NEXT VALUE OF X?'
         READ*, X
         PRINT*, 'F(X) IS ', F(X), ' FOR X = ', X
10    CONTINUE
      END

C This is the program for the function
      REAL FUNCTION F(X)
         REAL X
         IF (X.LT.0) THEN
            F = X * X
         ELSE
            F = X + 2.0
         END IF
      END
```

FIGURE 2.5.2
A Program using a function

```
PROGRAM MAIN
REAL  X, F
F(X) = X ** 3 + 2.0 * X * X
READ*, X
PRINT*, F(X)
END
```

FIGURE 2.5.3
Definition of a statement function

be REAL in a declaration statement. Once the function has been defined in this way, it may be used throughout the program just as an intrinsic or generally defined function. For example, statements such as those given in (2.5.3) may appear later in the program and will use the function definition as given in Figure 2.5.3.

Functions of several variables may also be defined. For example,

```
G(X,Y) = X * X + Y * Y
```

may be defined as a statement function. However, a function such as that given in Figure 2.5.1 may not be defined as a statement function, since it requires more than a single assignment statement for its definition.

Subroutines

A function is an example of a *subprogram*, an essentially independent program, but one that is always activated by another program. The other type of subprogram in Fortran is a *subroutine*. A function returns only a single value to the calling program, the value of the function. A subroutine, however, may return arbitrarily many values. A simple example of a subroutine is given in Figure 2.5.4.

The first line in Figure 2.5.4, which is the *calling sequence*, says that we are defining a subroutine named EXAMPL, with dummy (formal) arguments X, Y and Z. These formal arguments are declared (REAL, in this case)

```
SUBROUTINE EXAMPL(X,Y,Z)
  REAL X, Y, Z, W
 W = X + Y
 Y = (X * X) + W
 Z = (Y * Y) + SIN(X)
END
```

FIGURE 2.5.4
A subroutine

within the body of the subroutine; if other variables that are not arguments are used in the subroutine, they should be declared also, as is W. In this example, X is an *input variable*, and its value will be used to compute the *output variables* Y and Z. Y is an input variable, as well as an output variable. Note that the computation of Z calls the intrinsic function SIN. Other functions, for example the function of Figure 2.5.1, could have been called from within the subroutine. Generally, subprograms should perform tasks using the input variables and return values for the output variables. "Side effects" should be avoided. For example, input/output statements like READ and PRINT should not be used unless the subroutine is specifically designed for input or output.

Subprograms may be placed anywhere in the main program, but it is common practice to put them following the main program (as illustrated by the function in Figure 2.5.2). A subroutine is *called* from the main program, or from another subroutine, by a statement of the form

```
CALL EXAMPL(4.0, A, B)
```

In this case, X would take on the value 4.0, and A and B would play the roles of Y and Z. Thus, if A has the value 2.0 upon calling the subroutine, after the subroutine is done, A and B would have the values

$$A = (4.0)^2 + 6.0 = 22.0$$
$$B = (22.0)^2 + \sin(4.0) = 484.0 - 0.7568025 = 483.2432$$

Readability of the overall program is enhanced by using the same names for dummy and actual variables. Of course, if a subprogram is called different times with different actual variables, this is not possible.

Any variable that is defined within a subprogram and is not an argument in the calling sequence is *local* to the subprogram; that is, it is unknown to any other program. This is the case for the variable W in Figure 2.5.4: its *scope* is only the subroutine. Similarly, the scope of any variable in the main program is only the main program, and it is unknown to the subprogram unless it is an argument. In particular, there is no conflict in variable names so if W is an identifier in the main program, it is completely independent of the W in the subroutine. Similarly, the identifiers X, Y, and Z could be used in the main program without any conflict with their use in the subprogram.

Statement functions may also be defined within subroutines, and their scope is the same as local variables. Thus, a statement function defined in a subroutine cannot be used by the main program or another subroutine. Similarly, a statement function defined in the main program may be used only there and not by any subprogram. Note that this is not the case for functions defined by the general form of Figure 2.5.1. Such functions may be used by any *program unit*, that is, by the main program or by any other function or subroutine, provided that the function is compiled along with the calling unit.

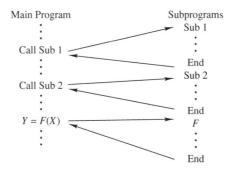

FIGURE 2.5.5
Control flow with subprograms

Flow of Control

Whenever a subroutine or general function is called, the main program transfers control to that subprogram. When the END statement is encountered in the subprogram, control is then passed back to the main program to the statement following the one that invoked a subroutine, or to the statement that called a function. This is illustrated schematically in Figure 2.5.5.

Advantages of Subprograms

The use of subprograms has several advantages. The first is that reprogramming may be avoided. For example, if the subroutine of Figure 2.5.4 is called at several different positions in a main program, the alternative would be to write the Fortran statements of the subroutine body each time they are used. More generally, subprograms lead to the possibility of *reusable* software, of which the Fortran intrinsic functions are a good example. Clearly, it would be very inefficient for everyone to start from scratch to compute the trigonometric functions, square roots, etc. Similarly, a subprogram that you write for some particular purpose might be usable in a different program by you or someone else. Other advantages of subprograms will be discussed in Section 2.7.

MAIN POINTS OF SECTION 2.5

- Fortran contains a number of intrinsic functions for mathematical operations, such as $\sqrt{x}$, $\sin x$, and so on.

- Additional functions may be defined by the programmer. A function subprogram may have only a single output value, which is assigned to the function name.

- Subroutines are more general subprograms that allow any number of variables as output.

- Functions that may be expressed by a single assignment statement may be defined as statement functions. Statement functions may be used only in the program unit in which they are defined.

- Subprograms enhance the possibilities of reusing software.

EXERCISES 2.5

2.5.1 Modify the volume program of Figure 2.2.1 so as to perform the computation of V in a subroutine or in a function.

2.5.2 Write general function subprograms that will evaluate the following functions. Make sure all variables are properly declared.

(a) $f(x) = (1 + x^2)/(1 + 3x^3)$
(b) $f(x) = (e^x \sin x)^4$
(c) $f(x) = \begin{cases} \sqrt{2x}, & \text{if } x \geq 0 \\ \sqrt{-x}, & \text{if } x < 0 \end{cases}$

Which of these functions may be defined as statement functions?

2.5.3 Write a subroutine that will compute the following quantities: $x = (y + w)^2$, $y = (x + w)^2$, $z = x^2 + y^2 + w^2$. State which are input variables for the subroutine, which are output variables, and which are both.

2.5.4 Write main programs that call the functions of Exercise 2.5.2 and the subroutine of Exercise 2.5.3. Make sure all variables are properly declared.

2.5.5 Run the program of Figure 2.4.5 for various values of X and EPS. Compare your approximations to EXP(X). Conclude that the larger X is, the more terms are needed in the series to obtain specified accuracy. Do the same for the cosine series of Exercise 2.4.6.

2.6

SCIENTIFIC COMPUTING: NUMERICAL INTEGRATION

We will now illustrate the Fortran constructs, as well as the general programming principles, that we have discussed so far. We will do this in the context of the numerical approximation of an integral[2]. This is a relatively simple but important problem that arises in many areas of science and engineering.

---

[2]If you have not yet studied integration, just consider the problem of approximating the area under a curve, as discussed in the text.

In calculus, we learn to integrate certain functions exactly, for example

$$\int_a^b x^3 dx = \frac{1}{4}(b^4 - a^4).$$

But most functions in real applications cannot be integrated in this "closed form" and the integral must be approximated. Indeed, in many applications there may not even be an explicit formula for f; rather, there may only be a table of function values at certain points in the interval, or a computer program that can calculate $f(x)$ for any x in the interval.

The integral

$$\int_b^a f(x) dx$$

may be interpreted as the area under the curve of f from a to b, as illustrated in Figure 2.6.1. An approximation to the integral may be obtained by introducing points $x_1, \ldots, x_n$ between a and b, as shown in Figure 2.6.1, then approximating the integral on each subinterval (x_i, x_{i+1}) by the area of an approximating rectangle or other simple geometric figure.

In Figure 2.6.2(a), the area under f from x_i to x_{i+1} is approximated by the area of the rectangle with height $f(x_i)$ and width $x_{i+1} - x_i$; thus

$$\int_{x_i}^{x_{i+1}} f(x) dx \doteq f(x_i)(x_{i+1} - x_i), \tag{2.6.1}$$

which is known as the *rectangle rule*. In Figure 2.6.2(b), the height of the rectangle is evaluated at the midpoint of the interval so that the approximation is

$$\int_{x_i}^{x_{i+1}} f(x) dx \doteq f\left(\frac{x_i + x_{i+1}}{2}\right)(x_{i+1} - x_i); \tag{2.6.2}$$

this is the *midpoint* rule. Still another approximation is shown in Figure 2.6.2(c) in which the area is approximated by that of a trapezoid, rather than a rectangle. In this case,

$$\int_{x_i}^{x_{i+1}} f(x) dx \doteq \frac{1}{2}[f(x_i) + f(x_{i+1})](x_{i+1} - x_i), \tag{2.6.3}$$

which is the *trapezoid* (or *trapezoidal*) rule.

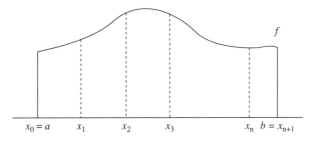

FIGURE 2.6.1
Integral as sum of areas

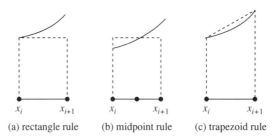

(a) rectangle rule   (b) midpoint rule   (c) trapezoid rule

FIGURE 2.6.2
Rectangle and trapezoid approximations

We will concentrate on the rectangle rule (2.6.1), but similar developments apply to the others (see Exercises 2.6.2 and 2.6.3). Using (2.6.1), the integral on the whole interval (a, b) is approximated by

$$\int_a^b f(x)dx = \sum_{i=0}^n \int_{x_i}^{x_{i+1}} f(x)dx \doteq \sum_{i=0}^n f(x_i)(x_{i+1} - x_i). \qquad (2.6.4)$$

For simplicity, we will assume that the points x_i are equally spaced with spacing h; that is, $x_{i+1} - x_i = h$ for $i = 0, \ldots, n$. Thus, (2.6.4) becomes

$$\int_a^b f(x)dx \doteq R(n) \equiv h \sum_{i=0}^n f(x_i). \qquad (2.6.5)$$

The larger n is the smaller h is and the more closely $R(n)$ should approximate the integral. In fact, under mild assumptions on the integrand f, it can be proved that

$$R(n) \to \int_a^b f(x)dx \quad \text{as } n \to \infty.$$

At the outset, we usually will not know how large n should be in order to obtain suitable accuracy in the approximation. Therefore, we will choose some reasonable $n = n_0$, and then compute the sequence of approximations

$$R_0 = R(n_0), \quad R_1 = R(2n_0), \quad R_2 = R(4n_0) \ldots, \quad R_i = R(2^i n_0), \qquad (2.6.6)$$

doubling the number of points each time. Note that h and n are related by

$$(n + 1)h = b - a; \qquad (2.6.7)$$

thus, each time we double n, we (approximately) halve h. We continue computing the approximations R_i of (2.6.6) until there is very little change between successive approximations. Thus, we continue until

$$|R_i - R_{i-1}| \leq \varepsilon, \qquad (2.6.8)$$

where ε is some chosen tolerance. We emphasize that because of finite precision arithmetic on a computer the parameter ε should not be chosen too small; this will be discussed further in the next section.

The problem now is to write a Fortran program to compute the sequence of approximations (2.6.6), where R is defined by (2.6.5), until (2.6.8) is satisfied. Before doing that, we will outline the overall structure of the computation by means of the flow chart in Figure 2.6.3. The program will require the integrand f, the end-points a and b of the interval of integration, the parameter ε of (2.6.8), and the initial number of points, n_0. The core of the computation is the evaluation of $R(n)$ by the formula (2.6.5). We will assume that this will be done by a subprogram and ignore the details of this computation for now. Similarly, we will not worry about the particular function f; we assume that it will be given by a function subprogram. Thus, we concentrate on the overall structure of the program. The main problem is how to handle the convergence, and one strategy for this is shown in the flow chart of Figure 2.6.3.

The first box in the flow chart shows the input information required. In the next box, $R(n_0)$ is computed and denoted by RC (for the current R). Then n is set to $2n_0$, and $R(n)$ computed and denoted by RN (for the next R). Now we begin a loop that will be repeated as long as two successive values of R differ by more than ε. Each time the loop is executed, n is doubled, RC is replaced by RN and a new RN is computed. When convergence occurs, we output the final approximation and the n for which that approximation was computed. Figure 2.6.3 uses a standard flow-chart convention: rectangles for assignment or computation, diamonds for decisions, trapezoids for input/output, and ovals for begin or end.

Next, Figure 2.6.4 gives a flow chart for the computation of $R(n)$. This flow chart is very simple and, perhaps, not even needed; the main advantage of flow charts is to show the logical flow of the program, especially when there are decisions to be made. Note that we still have not specified the function f to be integrated; this will be furnished by a separate function subprogram.

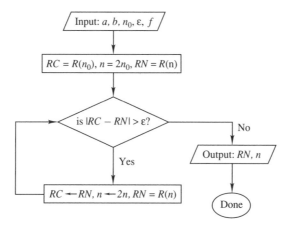

FIGURE 2.6.3
A flow chart for integration

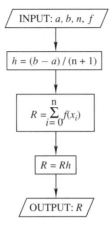

FIGURE 2.6.4
Flow chart for rectangle rule
subprogram

We are now ready to write the Fortran program by following the flow charts of Figures 2.6.3 and 2.6.4. Since the output of Figure 2.6.4 is a single number, R, we may elect to implement this either as a function or a subroutine. We have chosen a subroutine for illustration purposes, and this subroutine is given in Figure 2.6.5. The main Fortran program, as well as a function subprogram for a simple integrand, is given in Figure 2.6.6.

The main program in Figure 2.6.6 follows the flow chart of Figure 2.6.3 very closely. However, Figure 2.6.3 does not specify how the loop is to be implemented. We have done this by a WHILE DO construction, using the ABS intrinsic function of Table 2.5.1. (If your system has the DO

```
C     This subroutine computes a
C         rectangle rule approximation
      SUBROUTINE RECT(A,B,N,R)
         REAL A,B,R,F,H,X
         INTEGER N,I
         H = (B - A)/(N + 1)
         R = F(A)
         X = A
         DO 10 I = 1,N
            X = X + H
            R = R + F(X)
10       CONTINUE
         R = R * H
      END
```

FIGURE 2.6.5
A subroutine for the rectangle rule

```
***************************************************
* This program approximates an integral by       *
* using more and more points in the rectangle    *
* rule.  It requires a function subprogram        *
* for the integrand, the interval (A,B) of        *
* integration, an initial number of points,       *
* NO, for the approximation, and a                *
* convergence parameter, EPS                      *
***************************************************
      PROGRAM NUMINT
      INTEGER N0, N
      REAL A, B, EPS, RC, RN
C  Read input data after prompt
      PRINT*, 'A, B, NO, EPS = ?'
      READ*, A, B, N0, EPS
C  Now echo the input
      PRINT*,'A=',A, 'B=',B, 'NO=',N0, 'EPS=',EPS
C  Compute the first two approximations
C         to integral
      CALL RECT(A,B,N0,RC)
      N = N0 + N0
      CALL RECT(A,B,N,RN)
C  Check for convergence and repeat if not
      WHILE(ABS(RN - RC) .GT. EPS) DO
         N = N + N
         RC = RN
         CALL RECT(A,B,N,RN)
C  Display the results
         PRINT*, 'RN=', RN, '  N=', N
      END WHILE
      END
C  This defines a particular function to
C      be integrated
      REAL FUNCTION F(X)
         REAL X
         F =X/(1.0 + X * X)
      END
```

FIGURE 2.6.6
A Fortran program for numerical integration

WHILE construction instead, you must change the program accordingly.)
The subroutine RECT of Figure 2.6.5 carries out the rectangle rule. Note that
the computation of H mixes real and integer variables; this will be discussed
in Chapter 3. The main part of the subroutine computes the sum of the

function values, then multiplies this sum by h. An alternative formulation would be to multiply each $f(x_i)$ by h before summing, but this would be less inefficient than a single multiplication at the end. Moreover, these extra multiplications could introduce additional errors.

The function subprogram in Figure 2.6.6 defines a particular integrand. This subprogram would be replaced by whatever function you wish to integrate. Note that this function subprogram is called by the subroutine RECT, not the main program. Note also that the first statements of the program of Figure 2.6.6 are comments (where we have used * in column 1 rather than C). This provides an informative introduction to the program.

The program of Figure 2.6.5 and 2.6.6 produces the results shown in Table 2.6.1 for $a = 0, b = 1, n_0 = 2$, and $\varepsilon = .001$. The exact integral to five decimal places is

$$\int_0^1 \frac{x}{1+x^2} dx = \frac{1}{2} \log(x^2 + 1) \Big|_0^1 = \frac{1}{2} \log(2) = 0.34657$$

There are many possible modifications and extensions of the programs of Figure 2.6.5 and 2.6.6; some of these are explored in the exercise section. For example, the subroutine RECT could be replaced by another subroutine to carry out the midpoint or trapezoid rules shown in Figure 2.6.2. Both are, in general, better than the rectangle rule. (See Discretization Error in Section 2.7.) Exercise 2.6.4 gives still another approximation, Simpson's rule, that is even better. And OPEN and WRITE statements analogous to (2.2.4) could be added to the main program to prepare an output file that goes to a printer.

The program given in Figure 2.6.6 has some potential problems. First, it may give completely erroneous answers. This, and the general question of errors, will be discussed in Section 2.7. Second, it may not terminate if the ε chosen is too small. To guard against this possibility we should permit only a prescribed number of doublings of the number of points (or a maximum number of points to be used). We will see in Chapter 3 how to do this.

To summarize this section, we considered a relatively simple problem, numerical integration, and several possible approximations. We chose the

TABLE 2.6.1

Integral approximations

RN = 0.31777	N = 8
RN = 0.33158	N = 16
RN = 0.33892	N = 32
RN = 0.34271	N = 64
RN = 0.34463	N = 128
RN = 0.34560	N = 256

rectangle rule and constructed a flow chart showing the overall logic, ignoring the actual computations of the approximations. Based on this flow
chart, and a simple flow chart for the rectangle rule approximation, we then
constructed the final Fortran program. This program uses most of the Fortran constructs discussed so far: DO, WHILE, FUNCTION, SUBROUTINE,
and input/output statements.

One further comment is necessary. A program such as this would be
used to approximate integrals that can not be evaluated directly. However,
the program should be tested extensively on several integrands for which
the integral is easily computed. The more tests you perform, the more
confidence you will have in using the program for integrands with unknown
answers. Further discussion of program testing and detecting errors is given
in Section 2.7.

MAIN POINTS OF SECTION 2.6

- Many integrals in applications cannot be evaluated exactly and must
  be approximated numerically. Some simple methods for these approximations are the rectangle rule, the midpoint rule and the trapezoid rule.

- Before attempting to write a program, the overall logic of the program should be laid out. One way of doing this is by means of a
  flow chart.

- A program for numerical integration can consist of three parts: the
  main program handles input and output and convergence tests, a
  subroutine carries out the integration approximations, and a function
  subprogram defines the integrand.

EXERCISES 2.6

2.6.1 Type and run the program of Figures 2.6.5 and 2.6.6, and reproduce
the results of Table 2.6.1. How many points, N, are required to
obtain four decimal place accuracy?

2.6.2 The midpoint rule of Figure 2.6.2(b) and (2.6.2) leads to the approximation, corresponding to (2.6.6),

$$\int_a^b f(x)dx \doteq M(n) = h \sum_{i=0}^n f\left(\frac{x_i + x_{i+1}}{2}\right)$$

Replace the subroutine RECT in Figure 2.6.5 by one that carries out
the midpoint rule. Compute the points for which the integrand is
evaluated by using only one average, and then successive additions
of h.

2.6.3 The trapezoid approximation of Figure 2.6.2(c) and (2.6.3) leads to the approximation

$$\int_a^b f(x)dx \doteq T(n) = \frac{h}{2} \sum_{i=0}^{n} [f(x_i) + f(x_{i+1})]$$

$$= \frac{h}{2}[f(a) + f(b)] + h \sum_{i=1}^{n-1} f(x_i)$$

Replace the subroutine RECT in Figure 2.6.5 by one to carry out the trapezoid rule.

2.6.4 Another approximation is given by

$$\int_a^b f(x)dx \doteq \frac{h}{6} \sum_{i=0}^{n} [f(x_i) + 4f(\frac{x_i + x_{i+1}}{2}) + f(x_{i+1})],$$

which is *Simpson's rule*. Replace the subroutine RECT in Figure 2.6.5 by one that carries out Simpson's Rule.

2.6.5 Compare the accuracy of the rectangle, midpoint, trapezoid and Simpson's rule approximations on the integrand and parameters of Exercise 2.6.1 used for Table 2.6.1. Compare also the number of points, n, required to achieve convergence.

2.6.6 Add OPEN and WRITE statements to the program of Figure 2.6.6 to obtain an output file for a printer.

2.7

WRITING GOOD PROGRAMS AND DETECTING ERRORS

Refinement and Modularization

One of the biggest mistakes in programming is to begin writing the code before doing adequate planning. We should first make sure that we understand the "big picture" before attempting to write the final Fortran statements. An important paradigm for doing this analysis and planning is *top-down step-wise refinement*, in which the overall program is first outlined as to its major parts and logical flow. These major parts are then further broken down into subparts, and so on. Only after the problem is well understood and described in terms of a number of subtasks should the actual programming begin. We illustrated this procedure in Section 2.6, in which we first constructed a flow chart for the overall structure of the program, temporarily ignoring the details of the actual coding. Only at the end did we create the subprogram for carrying out the rectangle rule. In addition to flow charts, another useful tool to help in the break-down of the problem is *pseudocode*, which is a mathematical and English description of tasks to be done. Both flow charts and pseudocode will be used extensively in our discussion of scientific computing problems.

The process of top-down step-wise refinement becomes more important as the size of the program grows, and many problems in science and engineering require very large programs. For example, the NASTRAN program for finite element analysis has continued to evolve and expand for almost 30 years, and now contains several hundred thousand Fortran statements. This is an exceptionally large program, but it is not unusual for scientific and engineering programs to contain several thousand Fortran statements. It would be extremely difficult to write correct programs of this size without breaking them into smaller portions. This is sometimes called *modularization* of programs. Subprograms provide one mechanism for doing this as they allow the possibility of breaking up a large program into smaller units, each of which may be written and tested separately.

Structured Programming

Beginning in the 1960s, there was increasing concern about the difficulties being encountered in writing correct programs in a timely fashion. There was special concern about the difficulties in modifying existing programs, especially if the people doing the modifications were not the same people who wrote the programs originally. This was true because, in many cases, the program was almost impossible to understand. (Some programs became known as "spaghetti code", since the flow of control was so entangled.) Out of these concerns emerged a consensus about programming practices that would remedy these problems. These practices are principles of *structured programming*, and include the following:

- *Programs should be modularized.*
  Subprograms are a primary tool for this, although a module may also be a clearly demarcated section of a main program.

- *The flow of control should be clear and simple.*
  It has been the opinion of most of the computer science community for more than 20 years that the use of GO TO, or other branching statements, should be minimized, especially when the branch goes to a far away statement. Constructs such as IF/THEN/ELSE contribute to clear control flow. More generally, a program is *block-structured* if for any block of code there is only one entry to the block and only one exit from it.

- *Clear and meaningful names of variables and other identifiers should be chosen to follow the problem description as much as possible.*
  Cryptic variable names that have no relation to the problem should be avoided. Conflicts with standard mathematical notation should be avoided.

- *Use of programming "tricks" should be avoided.*
  Even though some tricks may be very clever and lead to better
  program efficiency, they can be counterproductive if they obscure
  understanding of the program.

- *The program should be well-documented.*
  Programs should begin with a beginning block of comment statements describing the purpose of the program, the input necessary,
  the output and so on. Additional comment statements should be used
  throughout the program to describe the purpose of the key parts.

We have already used several of these dictums, and we will continue
to do so throughout the book. Within the confines of these principles and
Fortran syntax, there is also the question of good *style*. Just as in writing
English, each programmer tends to develop a style of writing programs.
And, just as in writing English, one person's style may lead to programs
that have a pleasing appearance and are (relatively) easy to read, whereas
another person's style may lead to the opposite. Clearly, you wish to strive
for good style in your writing.

Errors

Even if you follow the previous guidelines for writing good programs,
it is inevitable that you will make errors. In Section 2.3 we mentioned
briefly the problem of errors in Fortran programs, and we now will discuss
this important concern in more detail. Errors in Fortran syntax are detected
by the compiler and are of two types. The first is a simple mistake of
misspelling a key word, for example, INTEGR, or omitting a "(", and so on.
These errors are usually very easily corrected. The second type of syntax
error arises by misunderstanding the language, for example, using identifiers
with too many characters or writing a DO loop in a way that is not legal.
Corrections of this type of error may require further study of the language.
Once the program has compiled correctly, there is then the possibility of
run-time errors, such as the attempt to divide by zero. Run-time errors
detected by the system are much like syntax errors and are usually easily
corrected.

A much more difficult problem, in general, is ascertaining if your
program is correct once no more syntax and run-time errors are detected by
the system. A first check is always for *consistency*: are the computed results
reasonable for the problem at hand? For example, if you are computing
the volume of a solid and the answer is negative, there is an error. Or,
if you are computing rocket trajectories that you expect to attain a height
of 5 kilometers, and your program is showing 500 kilometers, obviously
something is wrong.

Test Cases

Even if your program is computing reasonable results, that doesn't mean these results are correct. You should always run your program on several *test cases* for which you know the answer. For example, in the context of the integration program of Section 2.6, you should first test the function subprogram that evaluates the integrand. You might do this by calculating the integrand on a hand calculator for a few values of the argument and verify that your program reproduces these answers. Similarly, you should test the subroutine that computes the rectangle rule approximation, at least for small values of n. The more test cases you run successfully, the greater your confidence in the correctness of the program. In general, it is a good idea to test all of the subprograms first, before using them in a main program.

An important point is that many programs fail for very special conditions that may not be of much interest. For example, in Chapter 3 we will study the solution of N linear equations in N variables. It is easy to write programs for this problem that will fail for the trivial case $N = 1$. Thus, programs should also be tested for as many special case situations as possible.

Program Tracing by Hand

If your program results are not agreeing with your test case answers, the next task is to locate the error. If the program is sufficiently simple, a first approach is to follow the statements in the program by hand, doing exactly what the computer would do. A very simple example of this is the following. Suppose we wish to compute

$$a = b + c, \quad \text{if } c < 0$$
$$a = bc, \quad\quad \text{if } c \geq 0$$

and the corresponding program segment has the statements

```
IF (C. LE. 0) THEN
   A = B + C
ELSE
   A = B * C
END IF
```

Clearly, the program has an error, but it is a truism that many times a programmer can look repeatedly at a program and not detect an error that is obvious to someone else. However, by "tracing" the program, the error may be detected as follows:

CASE I. $B = 1, C = 1$. Then $A = 1$. (Correct)
CASE II. $B = 1, C = 0$. Then $A = 1$ by program. (Incorrect.)

You now recognize that `C.LE.0` should be `C.LT.0`. In realistic situations, the segment of the program that you're examining, and the error, will usually be much more complicated than this example.

Intermediate Output

Another standard way to attempt to isolate errors is to put `PRINT` statements in your program temporarily so that you can examine intermediate results. For example, suppose you suspect that there is an error in some particular `DO` loop, and you wish to examine what the results are as this loop is executed. This is illustrated in Figure 2.7.1.

The `READ` statement in Figure 2.7.1 causes the program to halt so you can examine the results on the monitor screen; hitting the ENTER(RETURN) key will resume operation. `READ*` is a "blank read" statement that calls for no data to be input, but still halts until the `ENTER` key is hit. Thus, you can step through this `DO` loop, examining the computation for each value of `I`. Once the program is correct you will remove the `PRINT` and `READ` statements. Fortran also has a `PAUSE` statement that has the same effect as the `READ*` statement, but the `PAUSE` statement is now considered by some to be obsolete.

Most Fortran systems will have an associated debugger program, which will allow you to examine intermediate results, and perform various other tasks, without inserting temporary statements into your program. You should become familiar with the debugger on your system.

Commenting Out

Another useful technique is to make comments out of certain statements in the program in order to deactivate them. Suppose, for example, that we are using the integration program of Figure 2.6.6 for the function shown in Figure 2.7.2, and we are obtaining erroneous answers. In order to run a test with a simpler function, we could change the function subprogram to that shown in Figure 2.7.3.

```
      DO 10 I = 1, N
         K = K + I * L
C This is a temporary print and pause
         PRINT * , I,K,L
         READ*
10       CONTINUE
```

FIGURE 2.7.1
A temporary PRINT

```
REAL FUNCTION F(X)
REAL X
   F = 32.0*X + 2.0*SIN(X) + 4.12*X**5
END
```

FIGURE 2.7.2
A function

```
        REAL FUNCTION F(X)
        REAL X
C          F = 32.0*X + 2.0*SIN(X) + 4.12*X**5
           F = X
        END
```

FIGURE 2.7.3
A new function with old one commented out

By adding the C in column 1 to the original function statement, this statement now becomes a comment, not an assignment statement. (Of course, without the C, the addition of the second statement for F has the same effect, but the C serves to mark a temporary change in this function.)

Rounding Error

Even if your program is "correct" you may still compute erroneous answers because of other, more subtle causes. One important source of error in any program that uses floating point arithmetic is *rounding error*. This is caused by the fact that computers work with only a finite number of digits. Because of this we cannot, in general, do arithmetic within the real number system as we do in pure mathematics: the arithmetic done by a computer is restricted to finitely many digits, whereas the numerical representation of most real numbers requires infinitely many. For example, such fundamental constants as π and e require an infinite number of digits for a numerical representation and can never be entered exactly in a computer. Moreover, even if we start with numbers that have an exact numerical representation in the computer, arithmetic operations using them will usually cause errors. In particular, the quotient of two numbers may require infinitely many digits for its numerical representation; for example, $\frac{1}{3} = 0.333\cdots$. And the product of two numbers will, in general, require twice as many digits as the numbers themselves, for example, $0.81 \times 0.61 = 0.4941$. These numbers must be truncated or rounded to the fixed number of digits we are carrying, for example, 23 bits. Therefore, we resign ourselves to the fact that we cannot do arithmetic exactly on a computer. We shall make small errors, called *rounding* or *round-off errors*, on almost all arithmetic operations, and we must ensure that these errors do not invalidate the computation.

Round-off errors can affect the final computed result in different ways. First, during a sequence of many operations, each subject to a small error, there is the danger that these small errors will accumulate so as to eliminate much of the accuracy of the final result. However, in most problems this is not as serious a danger as it might seem. More dangerous is the consequence of *cancellation*. Suppose that two numbers a and b are equal to within their last digit. Then the difference $c = a - b$ will have only one significant digit of accuracy even though no round-off error will be made in the subtraction. Future calculations with c may then limit the accuracy of the final result to one correct digit.

Whenever possible, one tries to eliminate the possibility of cancellation in intermediate results by rearranging the operations. We give a simple example of this using three-digit decimal arithmetic. Consider the computation of $AB - AC$ for $A = 1.12$, $B = 0.692$ and $C = 0.693$. Then,

$$AB = 0.775\underline{04} \quad AC = 0.776\underline{16}$$

where the underscored digits are lost when the results are rounded to 3 digits. Thus, the final computation gives

$$0.775 - 0.776 = -.001$$

as opposed to the correct answer, $-.00112$. However, suppose we had done the computation as $A(B - C)$. Then

$$B - C = -.001$$

so that

$$A(B - C) = -.00122. \tag{2.7.1}$$

Thus, there is no rounding error and we obtain the correct answer. (This is somewhat misleading, however. Suppose that the "true" values of B and C are $B = 0.69236$ and $C = 0.69294$, so that 0.692 and 0.693 are their best representations with three digits. Then the "true" answer is

$$A(B - C) = 1.12(0.69236 - 0.69294) = -0.00065$$

which differs considerably from (2.7.1).)

Discretization Error

Another source of error in many situations is the need to replace "continuous" problems by "discrete" ones. For example, the integral of a continuous function requires knowledge of the integrand along the whole interval of integration, whereas a computer approximation to the integral can use values of the integrand at only finitely many points. Hence, even if the subsequent arithmetic were done exactly, with no rounding errors, there would still be the error due to the discrete approximation to the integral. This type of error is called *discretization error*. All of the approximations to an integral discussed in Section 2.6 (rectangle rule, etc.) are subject to this type of error. In particular, for the rectangle rule approximation (assumed computed with no rounding error), the difference

$$h \sum_{i=0}^{n} f(x_i) - \int_a^b f(x)dx$$

is the discretization error.

In theory, we can estimate the error in the rectangle rule as follows. By the mean-value theorem

$$f(x) - f(x_i) = f'(z)(x - x_i)$$

where $z = z(x)$ is a point between x_i and x that depends on x. Thus, the error on the interval (x_i, x_{i+1}) is

$$E_i \equiv \int_{x_i}^{x_i+h} f(x)dx - hf(x_i) = \int_{x_i}^{x_i+h} [f(x) - f(x_i)]dx$$

$$= \int_{x_i}^{x_i+h} f'(z(x))(x - x_i)dx$$

Now assume that

$$|f'(x)| \le M \text{ for } a \le x \le b$$

Then

$$|E_i| \le \int_{x_i}^{x_i+h} |f'(x)|(x - x_i)dx \le M \int_{x_i}^{x_i+h} (x - x_i)dx = \frac{Mh^2}{2}$$

Thus, the total discretization error is bounded by

$$E = \sum_{i=0}^{n} |E_i| \le \frac{n+1}{2} Mh^2 = \frac{M(b-a)h}{2} \tag{2.7.2}$$

since $(n+1)h = b-a$. Because M and $b-a$ are fixed quantities, this shows that the discretization error goes to zero as h goes to zero or, equivalently, as $n \to \infty$, as expected.

In Section 2.6, the purpose of computing approximations $R(n)$ with larger and larger n was to make the discretization error smaller. However, the larger n is the more computation is done and the larger the rounding error is likely to be. Thus, we expect that there is a value of n for which the rounding error and discretization error are about equal, and no more progress can be made by taking n still larger. For most problems, this value of n will be considerably larger than is necessary to obtain suitable accuracy and the discretization error will still be the dominant component of the error. However, this discussion indicates a flaw in the program of Figure 2.6.6: if the value of ε is chosen too small (for example, 10^{-9}) the convergence test may never be passed because of the rounding error, and the program will not terminate. Thus, we should add another parameter that gives the largest number of iterations permitted. If this value is exceeded, the program will then terminate with a message that convergence was not achieved. In Section 3.2, we will discuss ways to add such a test to the program.

It is also possible for the convergence test used in the program of Figure 2.5.6 to fail completely. Consider the function shown in Figure 2.7.4, and suppose we start with $n = 1$. Then the first approximation by the rectangle rule is

$$\int_0^1 f(x)dx \doteq \frac{1}{2}f(0) + \frac{1}{2}f\left(\frac{1}{2}\right) = 1$$

For the second approximation, we double n to 2, and compute

$$\int_0^1 f(x)dx \doteq \frac{1}{3}\left[f(0) + f\left(\frac{1}{3}\right) + f\left(\frac{2}{3}\right)\right] = 1$$

Since two successive approximations are equal, the convergence test is satisfied. But, as evident from Figure 2.7.4, the exact integral is not at all equal to 1. This illustrates one of the many pitfalls that may occur in numerical computation.

Efficiency

The discretization error bound (2.7.2) for the rectangle rule is of the form ch, where c is the constant $M(b - a)/2$. This is many times denoted as $O(h)$, and we say that the error is of order h and the method is *first-order*. A similar but slightly more complicated analysis may be done for the trapezoid and midpoint rules, in which the error bound in both cases is a constant times h^2; we write this as $O(h^2)$ and say that the errors are order h^2 and that the methods are *second-order*. Generally, the higher the order of the method, the more *efficient* it will be; that is, less time will be required to compute an approximation to suitable accuracy.

Another important aspect of efficiency is that certain arithmetic operations take longer than others. Division always takes considerably longer than multiplication or addition. Thus, it is better to write $B*0.5$ than $B/2.0$. Similarly, on some machines, multiplication takes longer than addition, so that $B + B$ will be more efficient than $2.0*B$. (Good compilers will many times make optimizations such as this automatically.) We will consider

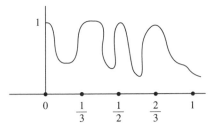

FIGURE 2.7.4
An integrand

throughout the remainder of the book the efficiency of algorithms, as well as of certain Fortran constructs.

MAIN POINTS OF SECTION 2.7

- Adequate planning should be done before writing a program. Top-down, step-wise refinement and modularization are paradigms for treating a program as a number of smaller tasks. These tasks may sometimes be conveniently implemented as subprograms.

- Structured programming is a paradigm for writing good programs by using modularization, clear control flow, good selection of variable names, avoidance of obscure programming tricks, and good documentation.

- Programs should be extensively tested to ensure that they do not have errors. Some tools for error detection are program tracing, intermediate output, and use of debuggers.

- Rounding error contaminates essentially all floating point computation. Especially dangerous are errors caused by cancellation.

- Discretization error results from solving a problem such as integration by a finite discrete approximation.

2.8

LOTS OF VALUES: ARRAYS

We now consider additional Fortran features. In Section 2.4, we discussed how to use a DO loop to repeat a computation many times. In the context of the volume computation of Figure 2.2.1, suppose that we wish to compute several values of V for given values of R, and then store these R and V values for further use. Each value of R would need its own storage location; we might give these values the names R1, R2, ..., with similar names for the V values. This has the disadvantage that we must declare lots of variables and we must decide in advance just how many values of R and V we wish to accommodate. This is very tedious; a much better way to handle this is by means of *arrays*. The declaration

        REAL A(100), B(100)   (2.8.1)

defines two arrays, A and B, consisting of 200 real *subscripted variables*: A(1), A(2), ..., A(100) and B(1), B(2), ..., B(100). That is, 200 positions for floating point numbers are reserved in memory, as indicated in Figure 2.8.1. In this figure, *a* is the beginning memory address of the array A. The elements of A are stored contiguously in memory one after

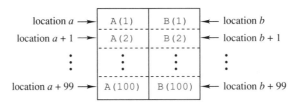

FIGURE 2.8.1
Memory allocation for arrays

another. The array B is stored beginning in memory address b, which is not necessarily the address $a + 99$.

Assuming that the elements of the array B have been assigned values (to be discussed shortly), the assignment statement

$$A(3) = B(3) * B(3) \tag{2.8.2}$$

will set A(3) to the square of the current value of B(3). But, rather then addressing some particular element of an array, as in (2.8.2), usually we will work with arrays in the context of DO loops, or other repetition constructs. For example, in place of (2.8.2), we would more likely be performing the computation for all values in the array, as illustrated by the program segment in Figure 2.8.2.

The declaration (2.8.1) reserves storage for 100 values of A and B, but all do not need to be used in any given instance. For example, (2.8.2) uses only one value of each, and the first statement in Figure 2.8.2 could be changed to

        DO 20 J = 1, 50

or

        DO 20 J = 1, N   (2.8.3)

where $N \le 100$. But in conjunction with (2.8.1), the statement

        DO 20 J = 1, 150

would be incorrect since values of A(J) and B(J) are not defined for J > 100. Most compilers would detect this error. However, if $N > 100$ in the

```
            DO 20 J = 1, 100
                A(J) = B(J)*B(J)
    20      CONTINUE
```

FIGURE 2.8.2
A DO loop with arrays

```
C This program computes the squares of
C     elements of an array
      PROGRAM SQUARE
      INTEGER J, N
      REAL A(100), B(100)
      PRINT*, 'WHAT IS N?'
      READ*, N
C Read the values of the array B
      DO 10 J = 1, N
         PRINT*, 'B(', J,') = ?'
         READ*, B(J)
  10     CONTINUE
C Compute and display the squares
      DO 20 J = 1, N
         A(J) = B(J) * B(J)
         PRINT*, A(J), B(J)
  20     CONTINUE
      END
```

FIGURE 2.8.3
Program with arrays and DO loops

statement (2.8.3), there will be an error when the program tries to access A(J) and B(J) for J > 100. In this case, the error is not detectable on compilation since the value of N has not yet been set. On some systems a run-time error message will be given if you attempt to access an array element outside its defined range, or if the array element has not yet been assigned a value. But on other systems, no error message will be given, and the program will simply use the erroneous data in the memory location. Figure 2.8.3 gives a simple, complete program in which, if a value of N exceeding 100 is read, then a run-time error or an erroneous result would occur in the subsequent DO loop when B(101) is addressed.

Figure 2.8.3 also illustrates the use of arrays in input/output statements. In the first DO loop, values for B(1), ...,B(N) are to be entered one at a time following the prompts. Each prompt will be of the form B(J) = ?, where the current value of J will be shown. Then, after the computations, pairs of values A(J) and B(J) are displayed on the monitor, one pair per line. There are a number of other, usually better, ways to perform input/output of arrays, as will be discussed in the next section.

Arrays and Subprograms

Array elements may be arguments of subprograms. For example,

Y = SQRT (A(3))

```
      PROGRAM MAIN
      INTEGER N
      REAL  A(100), B(100), S1, S2, ARSUM
      (Set values of A,B and N)
      S1 = ARSUM(A,100)
      S2 = ARSUM(B,N)
      PRINT*, S1, S2
      END

      REAL FUNCTION ARSUM(C,M)
        INTEGER I, M
        REAL C(M)
        ARSUM = 0
        DO 10 I = 1,M
          ARSUM =  ARSUM +C(I)
10        CONTINUE
      END
```

FIGURE 2.8.4
A function with an array argument

will compute the square root of the third element of the array A, assumed positive. Figure 2.8.4 illustrates that arrays themselves, not just a particular element, may also be arguments of a subprogram. This function computes the sum of M elements of an array called C in the function definition. In the first function call from the main program, the arguments are the array A and 100 for the value of M. Thus, the function ARSUM will compute the sum of all 100 elements of A. In the second call, the array is now B, and M is set to the current value of N. (The value of N as well as the elements of A and B are assumed to have been set by constructions, perhaps READ statements, not shown.) In this case, N may be any positive integer not exceeding 100, and the corresponding elements of the array B will be summed. Note that the declaration of C within the function uses the variable M. This is permissible within a subprogram, but in the main program actual numbers, as in (2.8.1), must be used in the array declaration.

Figure 2.8.5 gives another example of a subprogram with array arguments. This subroutine computes the n sums

$$c_i = a_i + b_i, \quad i = 1, \ldots, n. \tag{2.8.4}$$

This computation cannot be defined as a function since a function must have a single output number assigned to the function name, and (2.8.4) produces the n numbers $c_1, \ldots, c_n$.

The inputs to the subroutine of Figure 2.8.5 are A, B, and N, and C is the computed output. To invoke this subroutine in the main program one

```
        SUBROUTINE VECSUM(A, B, C, N)
           INTEGER N, I
           REAL A(N), B(N), C(N)
           DO 100 I = 1, N
             C(I) = A(I) + B(I)
100        CONTINUE
        END
```

FIGURE 2.8.5
Subroutine for (2.8.4)

would use a statement of the form

```
CALL VECSUM(X,Y,Z,100).
```

Here, 100 is the value of N and it is assumed that X, Y, and Z are arrays of size at least 100. The result of this call is that the array Z will contain the sums of the first 100 elements of the arrays X and Y.

Fortran 90

There are a number of significant differences in Fortran 90 regarding arrays, including dynamic storage allocation and array operations. These will be discussed in Chapter 4.

MAIN POINTS OF SECTION 2.8

- Arrays are a way to define subscripted variables such as $a_1, \ldots, a_n$.

- Arrays are usually used in conjunction with DO loops or other repetition constructions and may be arguments of subprograms.

- The lengths of arrays must be specified by numbers in the main program, but may be variables in subprograms.

EXERCISES 2.8

2.8.1 Run the program of Figure 2.8.3 for various values of N and B(1), ..., B(N).

2.8.2 Add an OPEN statement and a WRITE statement to the program of Figure 2.8.3 in order to produce a file for printer output.

2.8.3 Let $\mathbf{x} = (x_1, x_2, x_3)$ and $\mathbf{y} = (y_1, y_2, y_3)$ be two vectors starting from the origin in 3-space. The *dot product* (also called the *inner product*) of $\mathbf{x}$ and $\mathbf{y}$ is defined to be

$$(\mathbf{x}, \mathbf{y}) = x_1 y_1 + x_2 y_2 + x_3 y_3$$

Write a function subprogram to compute the dot product of two vectors **x** and **y**, where **x** and **y** are represented by arrays.

2.8.4 It is shown in analytic geometry that, in terms of the dot product of Exercise 2.8.3, the cosine of the angle between two vectors **u** and **v** is

$$\cos\theta = \frac{(\mathbf{u}, \mathbf{v})}{(\mathbf{u}, \mathbf{u})^{1/2}(\mathbf{v}, \mathbf{v})^{1/2}}$$

Write a main program that will read in two vectors **u** and **v**, and compute $\cos\theta$ by calling the function subprogram of Exercise 2.8.3 three times. Then compute the angle θ by using the intrinsic function ACOS (arc cosine). Finally, print the vectors **u** and **v** and the angle θ in degrees. Test your program for a number of vectors **u** and **v** for which you can easily compute the exact answers.

2.8.5 Two vectors **u** and **v** are *orthogonal (perpendicular)* if their dot product is zero. But because of rounding error, two vectors that are orthogonal may yield a non-zero computed dot product. We will say that the vectors are *numerically orthogonal* if $|\cos\theta| \leq 10^{-6}$. Add to your program of Exercise 2.8.4 a test to determine if two given vectors **u** and **v** are numerically orthogonal and, if so, print a suitable message to this effect.

2.8.6 Extend the programs of Exercises 2.8.3 – 2.8.5 to vectors **u** and **v** of length n. Declare the corresponding arrays in the main program to be as large as the maximum value of n you wish to consider.

2.8.7 The *mean* (average), $\bar{x}$, and *standard deviation*, σ, of n numbers $x_1, \ldots, x_n$ are defined by

$$\bar{x} = \frac{1}{n}\sum_{i=1}^{n} x_i, \qquad \sigma = \left[\frac{1}{n}\sum_{i=1}^{n}(\bar{x} - x_i)^2\right]^{1/2}$$

Write a subroutine that will accept n and the data $x_1, \ldots, x_n$ in the form of an array and return $\bar{x}$ and σ. Can you use your dot product subprogram of Exercise 2.8.6 in this problem?

2.9

NICER OUTPUT: FORMAT STATEMENTS

So far, our PRINT and WRITE statements have used only the *standard format*, which is sometimes called *list-directed* output. However, we can relatively easily set up any format we wish for our output by means of a *format statement*.

Consider the following statements:

```
      WRITE (7,100) X,Y                              (2.9.1a)
  100 FORMAT ('X =', F6.2, 'Y =', F8.3)             (2.9.1b)
```

In our previous WRITE statements, we used WRITE(7,*), the * signifying the standard format. Now we replace * by a statement number, 100 in (2.9.1a), that says the format will be defined by the FORMAT statement 100.

There are two ways to define the format of floating point numbers: the F-descriptor and the E-descriptor. The latter will be discussed in Chapter 3, and the F-descriptor is used in (2.9.1b). In general, descriptors define the width of the *field* in which a number (or set of characters) will be printed, as well as other information relevant to the entity to be printed. In particular, the F-descriptor has the form Fw.d, where d is the number of decimal digits to be printed to the right of the decimal point and w is the field width, which must be large enough to contain the d digits, the decimal point itself, and a position for a minus sign, if needed. For example, suppose that the current values of X and Y are -2.124569 and 33.51421. The statements of (2.9.1) would then produce a line of print of the form

```
      X = -2.12Y =   33.514                          (2.9.2)
```

Note that the labels 'X=' and 'Y=' defined in the format statement print as shown in (2.9.2). Note also that the number of digits to the right of the decimal point in X and Y is truncated to the number d in the F-descriptor, two in the first case and three in the second. Finally, numbers are *right-justified* in the field so that any blanks appear to the left of the number. Thus, there is one space after the X = in (2.9.2) since the descriptor F6.2 defines a field width of 6, and only 5 positions are used for the number. If the first descriptor in (2.9.1b) were changed to F8.2, there would be two additional blank spaces after X = in (2.9.2).

In order to use the F-descriptor it is necessary to know the magnitude of the numbers to be printed and allow suitable space. For example, suppose that the value of X is 4721.842. The descriptor F6.2 allows only three digits to the left of the decimal point, which is not enough to contain this value. Consequently, an error message will be printed, perhaps ***, saying that the number could not be printed in the space allowed. (We note that if enough space is available to print the digits but not a sign, positive numbers will be printed, but negative numbers will not. It is very poor practice to have the spacing this tight.)

Format statements can also be used with the PRINT statement. For example, in place of (2.9.1a) we could have

```
      PRINT 100, X, Y                                (2.9.3)
```

and the display on the monitor would be governed by the FORMAT statement of (2.9.1b).

It is also possible to put the descriptors directly in the PRINT and WRITE statements and not use a separate FORMAT statement. For example, the effect of (2.9.1b) and (2.9.3) could be achieved by the statement

$$\text{PRINT } '("X = ", \quad F6.2,"Y= ",F8.3)',X,Y \qquad (2.9.4)$$

Note that in (2.9.4), X= and Y= must be enclosed by ' ' rather than just ', as in (2.9.1b). The analogous construction can be used with the WRITE statement:

$$\text{WRITE } (7,'("X=",F6.2,"Y=",F8.3)') \ X,Y \qquad (2.9.5)$$

There are two advantages in using the FORMAT statement instead of the constructions (2.9.4) or (2.9.5). First, the same FORMAT statement can be used by more than one PRINT or WRITE statement. Second, the combination of the format specifiers in a single statement with the output list of variables may lead to overly complicated statements. In the future we will usually use the FORMAT statement, rather than constructions such as (2.9.4) or (2.9.5).

The I-descriptor

Printing of integers is controlled by a descriptor of the form Iw, where w is the width of the field. As with the F-descriptor, it is necessary to ensure that enough space is allowed for the size of the numbers expected. For example, assuming that I and J are integers with values I=421 and J=12, the statements

```
      PRINT 50, I, J
   50 FORMAT(I4, I3)
```

will produce the output

```
    421 12
```

Leading zeros will not be printed. If you want them to print, this may be achieved by the descriptor $Iw.m$, where m is the number of digits to be printed, including leading zeros. Of course, m must be no greater than w.

Spacing

The output line (2.9.2) has no spaces between Y and the previous number. Spaces could be added explicitly in the format statement; for example, if we changed ' Y=' in (2.9.1b) to '   Y=', two spaces would then appear before Y. An alternative is to use the the X-descriptor. If we change

(2.9.1b) to

```
100 FORMAT (10X, 'X=', F6.2, 5X, 'Y=', F8.3),
```

then 10 spaces will be added at the left of the line (useful for centering the output on the page, if desired) and 5 spaces will be added before Y in (2.9.2). Note that the X in the space descriptor has no relation to the variable X used in this example. An example combining the X, I, and F descriptors is

```
      PRINT 10, I, J, A, B
10 FORMAT (2X,I4,I3,2X,F6.2,F8.3)
```

If I=421, J=42, A=36.45, and B=829.413 when the PRINT statement is executed, the output line will be

```
bbb421b42bbb36.45b829.413
```

where the b's denote blanks.

We may also wish to control line spacing. An old Fortran convention is that the first character in the output line (that is, the sequence of characters to be printed) governs "carriage control" in the following way:

```
blank  – single space
  0    – double space
  +    – no space (overwrite)
  1    – new page
```

However, many printers will not respond to these codes and you may wish to ignore them. If so, it is customary to start the FORMAT statement with an X-descriptor, at least 1X, so that if your program runs on a system that obeys the carriage control codes, you will not get any surprises.

The way to control line-spacing is by means of a slash. For example, the format statement

```
100 FORMAT ('X=', F6.2 / 'Y=', F6.2)
```

will produce the two lines of print

```
X = -2.12
Y = 33.51
```

If you wish an extra line of space between these two lines, you can use // in place of /; in general, each / produces an extra line of space. Thus, the format statement

```
100 FORMAT (//// 'X=', F6.2, 'Y=', F8.3)
```

will give four blank lines before printing the line (2.9.2). This is useful in setting off different blocks of printing.

Printing and Reading Arrays

If A is an array of 3 elements, then the following statements are equivalent:

```
PRINT*, A(1), A(2), A(3)
PRINT*, (A(I), I=1,3)
```

The second statement uses an *implied* DO *loop*, with an integer variable I controlling the loop; this form is preferable for large arrays. The same construction may be used for read statements; for example,

```
READ*, (A(I), I=1,3)
```

will call for three values of the array A to be entered at the keyboard.
Another example is

```
       WRITE (7,100) (A(I), I=1,N)              (2.9.6a)
100 FORMAT(10X, 'OUTPUT' /(3F10.3))             (2.9.6b)
```

Here, it is assumed that A is a real array, and the value of the integer N in (2.9.6a) is no more than the length of the array. The format statement in (2.9.6b) illustrates two things. First, putting a number before the F-descriptor means replication of that descriptor. Thus, 3F10.3 is the same as writing F10.3, F10.3, F10.3. (The same replication can be done with the I-descriptor: 2I4 is the same as I4, I4.) Second, enclosing 3F10.3 in parentheses in (2.9.6b) means replication of these F-descriptors, if needed. For example, suppose that N=6 in (2.9.6a). Then, the output will be

```
        OUTPUT
   A(1)   A(2)   A(3)
   A(4)   A(5)   A(6)
```

where the actual current values of the A(I) would, of course, be printed. Thus, three values of A are printed on a line and a new line is started for the next three. Had the format statement in (2.9.6b) been

```
100 FORMAT(10X, 'OUTPUT'/6F10.3)               (2.9.7)
```

all six values of A would have appeared on the second line. On the other hand, if N=10 and (2.9.7) is used, then after the first six values of A are printed on the second line, the word OUTPUT would be repeated on the third line before the final four values of A were printed on the fourth line. This is different from the use of the format statement (2.9.6b) in which OUTPUT is printed only once, regardless of the size of N; this is because 3F10.3 was enclosed in parentheses. The general rule is that if more data remain to be printed after the format list is exhausted, then what was in the last set of parentheses in the format statement is replicated as the format information. In (2.9.7) there is only one set of parentheses, so the whole format statement is repeated.

Finally, we can also replicate parenthesized expressions. For example, 2(I4,F6.2) would be the same as I4, F6.2,I4,F6.2.

Tables

We can use the previous constructions to print tables in whatever form we desire. For example, suppose we have two arrays A and B and we wish to print a table that looks like

```
I A(I) B(I)
1 32.2 14.44
2 14.1 81.21
3 18.4 19.62
:   :    :
```

where the first line gives the headings. This could be accomplished by the statements

```
      WRITE (7,50) (I, A(I), B(I), I = 1,N)     (2.9.8a)
   50 FORMAT(5X,'I',5X,'A(I)',5X,'B(I)'
     + /(3X,I3,F9.1,F9.2))                       (2.9.8b)
```

The format statement (2.9.8b) begins with the header characters, followed by the descriptors for the numerical data. Since this sequence of descriptors is enclosed in parentheses, new lines will be produced as indicated in the table. The data specified in the WRITE statement must match this format; this is accomplished by the implied DO loop which indicates that the order of the data to be printed is 1, A(1), B(1), 2, A(2), B(2), ...

Files

In Section 2.2 we introduced the OPEN statement, which we now discuss in more detail. Historically, the READ and WRITE statements in Fortran referred to explicit input and output units, such as printers, card readers, tape units, and so on. Thus, in the statement

```
READ (5,*) X,Y
```

the number 5 referred to the card reader. Some of these conventions persist. For example, on some systems, in the statement

$$\text{WRITE}(6,*) \quad X, \ Y \tag{2.9.9}$$

the 6 refers to the monitor and (2.9.9) is equivalent to the statement

```
PRINT *, X,Y
```

The more modern convention is that the read and write statements usually refer to files, rather than specific input/output units. In principle, we could imagine that the statement

```
WRITE(OUT, *)   X,Y
```

would write X and Y to a file named OUT. Fortran, however, does not allow this construction. Rather, file names must first be associated with unit numbers: this is accomplished by the OPEN statement:

```
OPEN(UNIT, FILE=NAME)
```

Here UNIT is a nonnegative integer less than 100 and NAME is the name of the file. (Some systems may restrict the UNIT number from being certain reserved numbers, such as the 6 in (2.9.9)). For example, the statement

$$\text{OPEN}(12, \text{FILE} = ' \ \text{DONE} ') \tag{2.9.10}$$

opens a file named DONE and connects it to the program via unit number 12. Then any READ or WRITE statement in the program that refers to unit 12 will automatically read from, or write to, the file DONE. The OPEN statement must appear before any READ or WRITE statement that utilizes it.

This connection between unit number and file name will be broken when the program terminates, although the file may continue to exist; that is, after the program terminates, the results of the computation may reside on disk in a file named OUT and may be accessed by another program. The connection between a unit number and a file name also may be broken in the program itself by a close statement. Thus, the statement

```
CLOSE(12)
```

breaks the connection between unit 12 and the file named DONE. At this point, DONE is no longer connected to the program and may not be referenced by it unless another OPEN statement is utilized.

Fortran 90

One important change in Fortran 90 is that the FORMAT statement can be replaced by formatting information assigned to a character string. This will be discussed in Chapter 4, after character strings in Chapter 3.

MAIN POINTS OF SECTION 2.9

- Format statements allow customized output by specifying the number of digits to be printed, spacing, etc.

- The F-descriptor controls output of floating point numbers, the I-descriptor controls integers and the X-descriptor and / control spacing.

- Format information may be given in the `PRINT` or `WRITE` statements or referred to by a statement number.

- Arrays may be written or read by means of implied `DO` loops.

EXERCISES 2.9

2.9.1   Modify the volume program of Figure 2.2.1 in order to read N values of R, and put them in an array. Compute the corresponding N values of V, put them in an array, and output a table of values of the R's and corresponding V's.

2.9.2   Give the output of the following `PRINT` statement if A=41.12, B=-21.12, I=52, and J=101. Use b or _ for blank.

```
       PRINT 10, A, B, I, J
10     FORMAT(3X,F6.2,3X,F6.1,2X,2I2)
```

2.9.3   Show the output from the following `PRINT` statement for the values A=22.22, B=-11.1, C=33.333. Indicate blanks by b or _.

```
        PRINT 100, A, B, C
100     FORMAT (1X, 3F5.2)
```

2.10

SCIENTIFIC COMPUTING: DIFFERENTIAL EQUATIONS

Many problems in science and engineering ultimately can be reduced to solving *differential equations*[3] and solving such equations approximately is a very important problem in scientific computing.

In calculus, we learn how to solve simple differential equations such as

$$y'(t) = y(t) \qquad (2.10.1)$$

---

[3]If you have not yet studied differential equations, don't worry. You will only need to understand what a derivative is.

Here y is an unknown function of t and $y' = dy/dt$. The solution of (2.10.1) is

$$y(t) = ce^t \qquad (2.10.2)$$

for any constant c, as is verified by substituting (2.10.2) into (2.10.1) to produce the identity

$$ce^t = ce^t.$$

This example shows that the differential equation (2.10.1) by itself does not have a unique solution; rather, there is a family of solutions depending on a constant.

We may obtain a unique member of this family of solutions by requiring that the solution equal some specified value at some particular value of t. For example, if we require that the solution of (2.10.1) satisfy $y(0) = 3$, then the unique solution that achieves this is $y(t) = 3e^t$. In general, then, we will solve a differential equation subject to the requirement that the solution at some point t be given. This prescribed value of the solution is usually called an *initial* condition and the corresponding *initial value problem* is

$$\text{Solve } y'(t) = f(y(t)) \text{ subject to } y(a) = \alpha \qquad (2.10.3)$$

In (2.10.3), a is a given value of t, α is a given number, and f is a given function; for example, for (2.10.1), $f(y) = y$.

We were able to solve (2.10.1) explicitly because of its simple form, but this can not be done for most differential equations that arise in applications. Rather, we must approximate the solution, and we next consider some simple methods to do this.

Euler's Method

Suppose that $y(t)$ is the solution of the initial value problem (2.10.3). By definition of the derivative, we may approximate $y'(a)$ by

$$y'(a) \doteq \frac{y(a+h) - y(a)}{h} \qquad (2.10.4)$$

for sufficiently small h. Then, from (2.10.4), we have the approximation

$$y(a+h) \doteq y(a) + hy'(a).$$

Thus, knowing $y(a) = \alpha$ by the initial condition, we can approximate y at $a + h$ if we know $y'(a)$. We don't know the solution y, but from the differential equation we have

$$y'(a) = f(y(a)).$$

Therefore,

$$y(a+h) \doteq y(a) + hf(y(a)) \qquad (2.10.5)$$

is a computable approximation to $y(a+h)$.

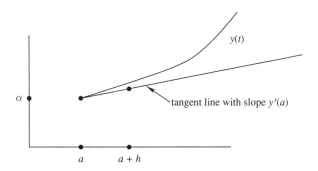

FIGURE 2.10.1
Approximation obtained from tangent line

We can represent the approximation (2.10.5) geometrically. As illustrated in Figure 2.10.1, the equation of the tangent line to $y(t)$ at $t = a$ is

$$T(t) = y(a) + y'(a)(t - a).$$

Thus, at $t = a + h$, and again setting $y'(a) = f(y(a))$,

$$T(a + h) = y(a) + hf(y(a))$$

so that the approximation (2.10.5) is the value of the tangent function at $a + h$.

Once we have the approximation at $a + h$, we may repeat the process to obtain approximations for additional values of t. Let

$$t_1 = a, \quad t_2 = a + h, \quad t_3 = a + 2h, \ldots, t_n = a + (n - 1)h \qquad (2.10.6)$$

and $y_1 = y(a)$. Then we may obtain approximations to the solution at the points (2.10.6) by

$$y_{i+1} = y_i + hf(y_i), \quad i = 1, \ldots, n \qquad (2.10.7)$$

This is *Euler's method*, the simplest method for approximating solutions of differential equations. A Fortran program for Euler's method is given in Figure 2.10.2.

The function used in Figure 2.10.2 is $F(y) = y$ so that for this function the program will approximate solutions of $y'(t) = y(t)$. If the initial condition is $y_1 = 1$, and $a = 0$, then the exact solution of the differential equation is e^t. The format statement 100 is written to print a table of t and the corresponding approximate solution. For $n = 5$ and $h = 0.25$, the output on the monitor will be

T	Y
0.00	1.0000
0.25	1.2500
0.50	1.5625
0.75	1.9531
1.00	2.4414

```
****************************************************
* This program approximates a solution to a     *
* differential equation y'=F(y) by Euler's      *
* method. The function F is assumed defined      *
* by a function subprogram. The initial          *
* point A, corresponding initial value y1,       *
* and the parameter H of Euler's method are      *
* input. The values of t and the solution        *
* are stored in arrays T and Y dimensioned       *
* as 100 long. Thus, N is restricted to no       *
* greater than 100 unless the array              *
* dimensions are changed.                         *
****************************************************
        PROGRAM EULER
        REAL T(100), Y(100), A, H
        INTEGER N, I, NM1
        PRINT*, 'VALUES OF A, N, H, Y(1) ARE:'
        READ*, A, N, H, Y(1)
        T(1) = A
        NM1 = N - 1
        DO 10 I = 1, NM1
          Y(I+1) = Y(I) + H*F(Y(I))
          T(I+1) = T(I) + H
   10   CONTINUE
        PRINT 100, (T(I), Y(I), I = 1, N)
  100   FORMAT(10X, 'T',9X,'Y'/(6X,F6.2,4X,F8.4))
        END

        REAL FUNCTION F(Y)
          REAL Y
          F = Y
        END
```

FIGURE 2.10.2
Euler's Method

Note that this approximation to e^t is very poor; in particular, the solution value for $t = 1$ should be $e = 2.71\ldots$. Next, we will discuss the reasons for this large error.

Errors

There are two types of errors in Euler's method. The first is rounding error, which may occur in the evaluation of $f(y_i)$, as well as in the multiplications and additions in (2.10.7). The second, and usually more serious error, is discretization error, which results from replacing the derivative by the approximation (2.10.4). The smaller h is, the more accurate is this approximation, and the smaller we would expect the discretization error to be. This is illustrated in Table 2.10.1 for the problem just discussed: $y'(t) = y(t)$ with $y(0) = 1$. Table 2.10.1 shows the approximate solution at $t = 1$, obtained by Euler's method with different values of h. The exact solution at $t = 1$ is $e = 2.718\ldots$ and the errors for the different values of h are given in the middle column.

As the *step-size* h decreases, the errors shown in Table 2.10.1 also decrease, as expected. The ratios of successive errors shown in the last column are decreasing more slowly, however. In fact, these error ratios will converge to $\frac{1}{2}$ as $h \to 0$. This is a consequence of the fact that the discretization error in Euler's method is proportional to h as $h \to 0$. Mathematically, we may write this as

$$|y_i - y(t_i)| \doteq ch, \text{ as } h \to 0, \tag{2.10.8}$$

where $y(t_i)$ is the exact solution of the differential equation at t_i, y_i is the Euler approximation at t_i and c is some constant. (The relation (2.10.8) is meant to hold at some fixed point $t_i = a + ih$, for example, the point $t = 1$ in Table 2.10.1. Thus, as $h \to 0, i \to \infty$ in such a way that t_i remains fixed.) Because of (2.10.8), Euler's method is called *first order* in h. A *higher-order* method will satisfy the relation

$$|y_i - y(t_i)| \doteq ch^p \tag{2.10.9}$$

for some integer $p \geq 2$, and p is called the order of the method. The higher the order, the more a decrease in h will decrease the discretization error. For example, if $p = 2$ and $h = .01$, then $h^2 = .0001$ so that the error is proportional to .0001, and not .01 as in Euler's method.

In practice, only high-order methods are used for solving differential equations, and Euler's method has been used in this section only as an illustration. A second-order method is given in Exercise 2.10.2.

Systems of Equations

We have considered methods for a single differential equation only, but for most applications we must solve systems of equations. Suppose that we have a system of first-order differential equations (only first derivatives

TABLE 2.10.1
Error in Euler's Method for $y' = y$ at $t = 1$

h	Computed Value	Error	Error Ratio
1	2.000	0.718	
1/2	2.250	0.468	0.65
1/4	2.441	0.277	0.59
1/8	2.566	0.152	0.55
1/16	2.638	0.080	0.53

are present), which we write in vector form as

$$\mathbf{u}'(t) = \mathbf{f}(\mathbf{u}(t)), \quad \mathbf{u}(0) = \mathbf{u}_0 \tag{2.10.10}$$

Here, there are n unknown functions $u_1(t), \ldots, u_n(t)$ with derivatives $u_1'(t), \ldots, u_n'(t)$, and n given functions $f_1(\mathbf{u}), \ldots, f_n(\mathbf{u})$. Then the vectors in (2.10.10) are

$$\mathbf{u}(t) = \begin{bmatrix} u_1(t) \\ u_2(t) \\ \vdots \\ u_n(t) \end{bmatrix}, \mathbf{u}'(t) = \begin{bmatrix} u_1'(t) \\ u_2'(t) \\ \vdots \\ u_n'(t) \end{bmatrix}, \mathbf{f}(\mathbf{u}(t)) = \begin{bmatrix} f_1(\mathbf{u}(t)) \\ f_2(\mathbf{u}(t)) \\ \vdots \\ f_n(\mathbf{u}(t)) \end{bmatrix} \tag{2.10.11}$$

We may now apply Euler's method (2.10.7) to the system (2.10.10) as

$$\mathbf{u}_{k+1} = \mathbf{u}_k + h\mathbf{f}(\mathbf{u}_k), \quad k = 1, 2, \ldots \tag{2.10.12}$$

Thus, by use of vector notation, Euler's method has exactly the same form as for a single equation. Of course, for computation we still need to use the components of the system. Thus, for $n = 2$, (2.10.12) would be written as

$$\left. \begin{array}{l} u_{1,k+1} = u_{1,k} + hf_1(u_{1,k}, u_{2,k}) \\ u_{2,k+1} = u_{2,k} + hf_2(u_{1,k}, u_{2,k}) \end{array} \right\} k = 1, 2, \ldots \tag{2.10.13}$$

A Predator-Prey Problem

As an example of how a system of differential equations arises, we consider the interaction of two species that have a predator-prey relationship. We assume that the prey is able to find sufficient food, but is killed by the predator whenever they encounter each other. Examples of such species interactions are wolves and rabbits, and parasites and certain hosts. We want to investigate how the predator and prey populations vary with time.

Let $v(t)$ and $w(t)$ designate the number of prey and predators, respectively, at time t. To derive mathematical equations relating v and w, we make several simplifying assumptions. First, we assume that the prey's birth rate, v_b, and natural death rate (exclusive of predator killing), v_d, are constant with $v_b > v_d$. Thus, the prey population, if left alone, increases at the rate $(v_b - v_d)v$. Second, we assume that the number of kills the predator makes depends on the probability of the predataor and prey coming together and is therefore proportional to vw. Combining these two assumptions, the prey population is governed by the differential equation

$$v'(t) = \alpha v(t) + \beta v(t)w(t) \tag{2.10.14a}$$

where $\alpha \equiv v_b - v_d > 0$ and $\beta < 0$.

In order to derive the predator equation, we assume that the number of predators would decrease by natural causes if the prey were removed, contributing a γw term. However, the number of predators increases as a result of encounters with prey, leading to

$$w'(t) = \gamma w(t) + \delta v(t)w(t) \qquad (2.10.14b)$$

with $\gamma < 0$ and $\delta > 0$. In addition to these differential equations, we will have the initial conditions

$$v(0) = v_1, \quad w(0) = w_1$$

where v_1 and w_1 are the initial populations of the prey and the predators. Euler's method for the equations (2.10.14) is then obtained by taking $v = u_1$ and $w = u_2$ in (2.10.13), with the functions

$$f_1(\mathbf{u}) = \alpha u_1 + \beta u_1 u_2, \qquad f_2(\mathbf{u}) = \gamma u_2 + \delta u_1 u_2 \qquad (2.10.14)$$

Thus, Euler's method for (2.10.14) is

$$\left.\begin{array}{l} v_{k+1} = v_k + h(\alpha v_k + \beta v_k v_k) \\ w_{k+1} = w_k + h(\gamma w_k + \gamma v_k w_k) \end{array}\right\} k = 1, 2, \ldots \qquad (2.10.15)$$

A Fortran program to carry out (2.10.16) is given in Figure 2.10.3. In this program we have denoted the number of prey, v, by PREY, and the predators, w, by PRED. The program sets α, β, γ, and δ by parameter statements, reads in the value of h and the number, n, of Euler steps to take as well as the initial conditions for PREY and PRED. (Note that more than one value may be set in a parameter statement, as opposed to the single value in Figure 2.2.1.) The DO loop successively computes and prints the Euler approximations, rather than saving them in arrays as in Figure 2.10.2. Note that since the current values of PREY and PRED are used in the temporary variable P, they may be overwritten by the new values as they are computed.

Exercise 2.10.3 asks you to obtain approximate solutions of the predator-prey equations by running the program of Figure 2.10.3 for various values of h. Exercise 2.10.5 considers another system of differential equations, which model the trajectory of a projectile (for example, a cannon shell) that starts with some initial velocity and launch angle. This is a special case of the more general problem of computing rocket trajectories.

Modeling Error

Another very important type of error is not caused by errors in the computation, but in the formulation of the problem. Many computational problems in science and engineering are *simulations* of some physical process. Examples of this are rocket or spacecraft trajectories, air flow over an aircraft, blood flow in the human body, and so on. Such phenomena may be described by a *mathematical model*, which is usually one or more differential equations. The predator-prey problem and the trajectory problem of Exercise 2.10.5 are examples of such mathematical models.

The formulation of a mathematical model begins with a statement of factors to be considered. In many physical problems, these factors concern

```
*****************************************************
* This program obtains an approximate solution *
* by Euler's method to the equations (2.10.4)  *
* for given values of alpha, beta, gamma and   *
* delta and given initial values of the        *
* solutions PREY and PRED.                      *
*****************************************************
      PROGRAM PRPR
      REAL H,PREY,PRED,P,ALPHA,BETA,GAMMA,DELTA
      INTEGER I, N
      PARAMETER(ALPHA = 0.25, BETA = -0.01)
      PARAMETER(GAMMA = -1.0, DELTA = 0.01)
      PRINT, 'WHAT ARE VALUES OF H AND N?'
      READ*, H, N
      PRINT*, 'WHAT ARE INITIAL VALUES?'
      READ*, PREY, PRED
      DO 1 I = 1,N
*     The product of current PREY and PRED
*        is saved
      P = PREY * PRED
      PREY = PREY + H*(ALPHA*PREY + BETA*P)
      PRED = PRED + H*(GAMMA*PRED + DELTA*P)
*     Print current values of time, ih, and
*        PREY and PRED
      PRINT *, I * H, PREY, PRED
1     CONTINUE
      END
```

FIGURE 2.10.3
Euler's Method for predator-prey equations (2.10.14)

the balance of forces and other conservation laws of physics. For example, in the formulation of a model of a trajectory the basic physical law is Newton's second law of motion, which requires that the forces acting on a body equal the rate of change of momentum of the body. This general law must then be specialized to the particular problem by enumerating and quantifying the forces that will be important. For example, the gravitational attraction of Jupiter will exert a force on a rocket in Earth's atmosphere, but its effect will be so minute compared to the earth's gravitational force that it can be neglected. Other forces may also be small compared to the dominant forces, but their effects might not be so easily dismissed; the construction of the model will invariably be a compromise between retaining all factors that could likely have a bearing on the validity of the model and keeping the mathematical model sufficiently simple so that it can be solved using the tools at hand. Historically, only very simple models of most phenomena were considered since the solutions had to be obtained by hand, either analytically or numerically. As the power of computers and numerical methods have developed, increasingly complicated models have become tractable. However, all such models will only be an approximation to physical reality.

MAIN POINTS OF SECTION 2.10

- Differential equations need initial conditions in order that a unique solution can be determined.

- Approximate solutions of differential equations may be obtained by replacing derivatives by approximations. Euler's method is the simplest method so obtained.

- Many applications require the solution of a system of differential equations. Examples are the predator-prey equations and the equations of rocket trajectories. Euler's method is easily extended to systems of equations.

- Discretization error and rounding error affect the accuracy of approximate solutions. Discretization error is usually the more serious. There is also modeling error in setting up the differential equations.

EXERCISES 2.10

2.10.1 Run the program of Figure 2.10.2 with values of h and n chosen in order to reproduce the values in Table 2.10.1.

2.10.2 The second-order Runge-Kutta method for the initial value problem (2.10.3) is given by

$$y_{i+1} = y_i + \frac{h}{2}[f(y_i) + f(y_i + hf(y_i))], \quad i = 1, 2, \ldots$$

Modify the program of Figure 2.10.2 to carry out this method. Run your program for the problem (2.10.1) with $y(0) = 1$, and compare your results with Euler's method. In particular, compare the accuracy of an approximation to e, as done in Table 2.10.1, for the same value of h in both programs.

2.10.3 Run the program of Figure 2.10.3 for the initial values $v(0) = 80, w(0) = 30$, and for various values of h, for example, $h = 1, .5, .25$. The exact solution of the equations (2.10.14) is almost periodic for the given values of α, β, δ, and γ, and the initial conditions. How small do you need to take h before you begin to see this almost periodic behavior? If you have access to a graphics system, plot the solution in the v, w plane.

2.10.4 The second-order Runge-Kutta method of Exercise 2.10.2 may be written for the system (2.10.10) as

$$\mathbf{u}_{i+1} = \mathbf{u}_i + \frac{h}{2}[\mathbf{f}(\mathbf{u}_i) + \mathbf{f}(\mathbf{u}_i + h\mathbf{f}(\mathbf{u}_i))], i = 1, 2, \ldots$$

Write this out explicitly for two equations, and then write a Fortran program to carry out this method for the predator-prey equations (2.10.14). For the same values as in Exercise 2.10.3, compare the accuracy with Euler's method. For what values of h do you begin to see the almost periodic behavior of the solution using the Runge-Kutta method?

2.10.5 The trajectory of a short-range projectile may be modeled by the following system of four differential equations:

$$x'(t) = v(t)\cos\theta(t), \qquad y'(t) = v(t)\sin\theta(t)$$
$$v'(t) = -\alpha[v(t)]^2 - g\sin\theta(t), \quad \theta'(t) = [-g\cos\theta(t)]/v(t).$$

Here, $x(t)$ and $y(t)$ are the coordinates of the projectile at time t, $v(t)$ is the velocity, $\theta(t)$ is the angle from the horizontal, g is the gravitational force, and α is a constant depending on air density, the coefficient of drag, mass, and cross-sectional area of the projectile. Euler's method for this system of differential equations is

$$\left.\begin{array}{l} x_{k+1} = x_k + hv_k\cos\theta_k \\ y_{k+1} = y_k + hv_k\sin\theta_k \\ v_{k+1} = v_k - h(\alpha v_k^2 + g\sin\theta_k) \\ \theta_{k+1} = \theta_k - h\frac{g}{v_k}\cos\theta_k \end{array}\right\} k = 1, 2, \ldots$$

where $x_1 = y_1 = 0$ are the initial coordinates of the projectile, v_1 is the prescribed initial velocity, and θ_1 is the prescribed launch angle in radians. Let $g = 9.81$ and $\alpha = 0.00215$, and write a program to carry out Euler's method.

(a)   If there is no drag, then $\alpha = 0$ and the differential equations have the exact solutions

$$x(t) = (v_1\cos\theta_1)t$$
$$y(t) = (v_1\sin\theta_1)t - gt^2/2$$

Use this as a test case with the initial conditions $v_1 = 50$ m/sec and $\theta_1 = 0.6$ radians. Find a value of h that makes the computed solution accurate to about 2 decimal places.

(b)   For the original value of α, $v_1 = 50$, and the h you determined in part a, find a value of θ_1 so that the projectile hits the ground at 125 meters. If you have access to a graphics system, plot this trajectory.

3

EXTENSIONS AND RESTRICTIONS

In Chapter 2, we described the basic Fortran constructs. In most cases there are extensions of these constructs that are useful for more general situations. There are also various restrictions and rules that must be followed; we downplayed these in Chapter 2 because we wished to emphasize the basic simplicity of the language.

3.1

EXPRESSIONS, TYPES AND DATA

In Chapter 2, we used only very simple arithmetic expressions. We now wish to discuss what is permissible, what is not permissible, and what is permissible, but poor practice.

Exponentiation

We noted that R^3 may be written as R**3 in Fortran. In general, we can write R**I for any real or integer variable R and any integer I. We can also write R**S, where S is real; for example

$$R**0.5, \quad R**3.5, \quad R**7.1 \tag{3.1.1}$$

The first of these expressions is just another way to write $\sqrt{R}$, rather than SQRT(R). Similarly, R**3.5 is $R^{7/2}$, which could be written as

SQRT(R)**7. The SQRT function requires that its argument have only nonnegative values and this same restriction applies to the exponentiations of (3.1.1). Hence, we have the following restriction:

> For an exponentiation R**S, where R and S are real,   (3.1.2)
> R must be nonnegative.

This restriction does not apply if S is an integer since R^S is well-defined in this case, no matter whether R is positive or negative. However, if R is negative and you write

$$R**3.0 \qquad\qquad (3.1.3)$$

rather than R**3, this will violate (3.1.2), since the decimal point in 3.0 defines it to be a real constant instead of an integer constant.

We note that exponentiation is more time-consuming than basic arithmetic operations. Thus, for example, it is more efficient to write R*R*R than (3.1.3). (Some compilers may recognize that R**3 may be evaluated by multiplications.)

Operator Precedence

When we write R*R*R there is no ambiguity. But with the expression A/B*C we could mean either

$$(A/B)*C \qquad \text{or} \qquad A/(B*C) \qquad\qquad (3.1.4)$$

Fortran resolves this ambiguity by the following *operator precedence*:

$$**, \quad /, \quad *, \quad \pm; \qquad\qquad (3.1.5)$$

that is, exponentiation is always performed first, followed by division, then multiplication, and finally addition and subtraction. Thus, Fortran would treat A/B*C as equivalent to the first form of (3.1.4). Some other examples are:

$$A + B * C \qquad \text{is same as} \qquad A + (B * C) \qquad\qquad (3.1.6a)$$

$$A * *3 * C \qquad \text{is same as} \qquad (A * *3) * C \qquad\qquad (3.1.6b)$$

$$A * B + A/B \qquad \text{is same as} \qquad (A * B) + (A/B) \qquad\qquad (3.1.6c)$$

In general, arithmetic expressions can be evaluated in any order subject to the operator precedence (3.1.5), although parentheses override this precedence.

Even though Fortran resolves the ambiguities in arithmetic expressions by means of the operator precedence (3.1.5), it is bad practice to rely exclusively on this precedence: *Ambiguities should usually be resolved by using parentheses.* This has the advantage that neither you nor someone else reading your program need worry about remembering the precedence, there is less chance for error, and the statements will be clear as written. Thus, for example, you should always use the second form in (3.1.6), rather than the first form. However, long and complicated expressions should be broken up into shorter expressions rather than using numerous parentheses. For example, with an expression like

```
Z = (A+B)**3/(B+C)*C*A/D*B+A**2/C
```

the addition of parentheses would make the computation less clear than breaking it up as

```
X = ((A+B)**3)/(B+C)
Y = (X*C*A)/D
Z = (Y*B)+(A**2)/C
```

With expressions such as A*B*C or A+B+C there is no ambiguity, therefore no need to use extra parentheses. However, with A/B/C there are the two possibilities

$$(A/B)/C \quad \text{or} \quad A/(B/C) . \tag{3.1.7}$$

Fortran resolves this ambiguity by evaluating the divisions left to right, so that the first expression in (3.1.7) would be computed. Note, however, that

$$(A/B)/C = A/(B*C) \tag{3.1.8}$$

and since on most machines division is much slower than multiplication, the second form of (3.1.8) is preferred. (Some compilers will indeed evaluate A/B/C by means of the second form of (3.1.8)).

Mixing Types

Mixing integer and real variables in the same expression is allowed, but not recommended. Explicitly declaring all variables and not mixing types in the same expression is called *strong typing*, and is the recommended practice. However, it is common to mix types, and to be able to read existing programs that do this there are some rules that must be understood. In the following discussion, we assume that I and J are integers and A, B, and C are real.

As a first example, in the statement

```
C = A+I
```

I is first converted to real, and then the addition performed and the corresponding real value assigned to C. The conversion of I is only for the computation; I remains an integer in memory and may be used later as such. In the statement

```
C = A**I
```

I is *not* converted to real since, by our previous discussion of exponentiation, this would lead to an error if A were negative. The general rule is:

> *If integers and reals are mixed in an arithmetic expression, all integer values are temporarily converted to real for the computation, except in the case of an integer exponent.*

Another type of situation is the following. In the statement,

```
I = A+B
```

the computation is done in floating point arithmetic and the result is truncated to an integer. For example, if A=3.2 and B=2.4, then A+B =5.6 and I is assigned the integer value 5. Similarly, in the statement

```
C = I * J
```

the multiplication is performed in integer arithmetic, and the result is then converted to real for assignment to C.

The corresponding statement with division leads to potential difficulties. In

$$C = I/J \tag{3.1.9}$$

the division is done in integer arithmetic, and the result is the integer part of the quotient; that is, there is no rounding. Thus, if I = 5 and J=3, the quotient is $1.666\cdots$, whose integer part is 1; this is the value assigned to C, rather than the correctly rounded one. Another example is that whenever I > 1

$$I * (1/I) \neq 1$$

since the quotient will be computed to be zero.

If your intention in (3.1.9) is to assign to C the correct quotient, rather than just its integer part, you can write in place of (3.1.9)

$$C = REAL(I)/REAL(J) \tag{3.1.10}$$

In (3.1.10), REAL(I) is an intrinsic function whose value is the floating point representation of I. (FLOAT is another name for this intrinsic function.) Then, the division in (3.1.10) is performed in floating point arithmetic and the correct quotient assigned to C. A related intrinsic function is NINT, which converts a floating point number to the correctly rounded integer. For example, if A=3.5, NINT(A)=4. INT is another intrinsic function that truncates a floating point number to an integer; thus, INT(3.5)=3.

Double Precision

As discussed in Chapter 1, on many computers, especially PCs, a floating point number is represented by 32 bits, with 23 or 24 bits for the mantissa. This corresponds to approximately seven decimal digits of precision, and for some computations this may not be sufficient. *Double precision* numbers will allow twice the number of bits for a floating point number. Thus, if 32 bits are used for "standard" floating point numbers, called *single precision*, then 64 bits will be used for double precision. Depending on the particular machine, at least 48 of these bits will be allocated to the mantissa, allowing precision of at least 14 decimal digits. (On some large computers, single precision is already 64 bits, so double precision is 128 bits.)

To handle double precision numbers, Fortran allows a corresponding type declaration. Thus, the statement

```
DOUBLE PRECISION X, Y, A(10)
```

declares X, Y, and all elements of the array A, to be double precision. Functions may also be declared double precision; for example,

```
DOUBLE PRECISION FUNCTION F(X)
```

Mixing double precision and real types in an arithmetic expression is permissible, with rules similar to those for mixing real and integer variables. Now, however, double precision takes precedence. For example, suppose that X has been declared REAL and Y has been declared DOUBLE PRECISION. Then, in the expression

```
X = X + Y
```

the addition will be done in double precision and the result rounded to single precision for assignment to X.

Double precision arithmetic is implemented by software on many machines and may be considerably slower than single precision. Double precision numbers also require twice the memory of those that are single precision. Therefore, double precision should only be used if the need for it is clear, or if the additional time and memory are unimportant. One common way to ascertain if double precision is necessary is to run some trial cases in both single and double precision. If there is no meaningful difference in the result, to the accuracy desired, double precision is not necessary.

Complex Numbers

Suppose that

$$a = \alpha + i\beta, \quad b = \gamma + i\mu$$

are complex numbers with $\alpha, \beta, \gamma, \mu$ real and $i = \sqrt{-1}$. The rules for addition and multiplication of complex numbers are

$$a + b = (\alpha + \gamma) + i(\beta + \mu)$$
$$ab = (\alpha + i\beta)(\gamma + i\mu) = (\alpha\gamma - \beta\mu) + i(\beta\gamma + \alpha\mu) \tag{3.1.11}$$

These formulas for the real and imaginary parts of the sum and product could, of course, be programmed in Fortran. However, Fortran allows complex variables to be declared by the statement

```
COMPLEX A, B, C
```

After this declaration the arithmetic operations of (3.1.11) can be achieved by

```
C = A + B,        C = A * B
```

and the real arithmetic of (3.1.11) will be carried out automatically to give the proper complex results. As might be expected, complex numbers in Fortran are represented by two real numbers in storage. Thus, the complex number $2.0 + 4.0i$ will be the pair $(2.0, 4.0)$, and a corresponding assignment statement will assign this value to the variable C:

```
C = (2.0, 4.0)
```

Complex functions and arrays may also be declared. For example,

```
COMPLEX C(10)
```

defines C to be an array of 10 complex numbers, and

```
COMPLEX FUNCTION G(Z)
```

defines G to be a function that will take on complex values. Printing of complex numbers may be achieved by, for example,

```
        PRINT 100, C
100     FORMAT(10X, 2F6.2)
```

Here, note that 2F6.2 is specified since C will be printed as two real numbers. Finally, exponentiation with complex numbers is permitted, except that some systems may not accept

$$C ** A \tag{3.1.12}$$

if C is complex and A is real or complex, even though this can be defined mathematically. Exponentiation of complex numbers is always permitted for integers; that is, when A is an integer in (3.1.12). On the other hand, the SQRT intrinsic function will accept complex arguments; also, the square root of a negative number is permitted if that number has been declared as complex.

Data Specification

In the volume program in Chapter 2, we defined a constant PI by the statement

$$PARAMETER \ (PI = 3.1415927) \tag{3.1.13}$$

Any number of constant values may be defined by a PARAMETER statement; for example,

$$PARAMETER \ (A= 3.0, \ B= 4.5, \ I =3) \tag{3.1.14}$$

sets A, B, and I to the indicated values. (Recall that we used such statements in the program of Figure 2.10.3.) It is assumed in (3.1.14) that A, B, and I have already been declared as REAL or INTEGER. It is considered good practice to collect all parameters of a program together in one or more PARAMETER statements at the beginning of the program after type declarations, rather than scatter assignment statements throughout the program.

Another way to specify numerical values is by means of the DATA statement. For example,

$$DATA \ A/3.0/, \ B/4.5/, \ I/3/ \tag{3.1.15}$$

assigns the values 3.0, 4.5, and 3 to A, B, and I, respectively. A major difference between the DATA and PARAMETER statements is that a variable set by a PARAMETER statement cannot be changed in the course of the program. For example, if I is set by (3.1.14), then a statement like

$$I = I + 2$$

is not permitted. On the other hand, the DATA statement is usually used to initialize values of variables that may change during subsequent calculations.

Moreover, it is much more flexible than indicated by (3.1.15). For example, the statements

```
REAL A(100), B(100)                          (3.1.16)
DATA A/100 * 0/, B/50*2.0, 50*1.0/
```

will assign the value 0 to all 100 elements of the array A, 2.0 to the first 50 elements of B and 1.0 to the last 50. More generally, we may use implied DO loops within DATA statements. If A is again declared by (3.1.16), the statement

```
DATA (A(I), I = 26,50) / 25*1.5/            (3.1.17)
```

will assign 1.5 to elements A(26) through A(50).

For both the PARAMETER and the DATA statements, the assignment of values is done at compilation, and all DATA statements must appear before any executable statement, but after type declarations.

Fortran 90

The DOUBLE PRECISION declaration becomes obsolete because other constructs allow specification of precision. Also, the DATA statement becomes somewhat obsolete. Both points will be discussed in Chapter 4, as well as the definition of "derived types."

MAIN POINTS OF SECTION 3.1

- Exponentiation, R**S, is allowed for any real R if S is integer, but only for nonnegative R if S is real.

- Expressions are evaluated using the operator precedence $**, /, *, \pm$. Parentheses override this precedence. Parentheses should be used to make the order of operations clear without relying on precedence.

- If integer and real variables are both used in an arithmetic expression, the integers are temporarily converted to real for the computation, except in the case of an integer exponent.

- Double precision and complex are two additional data types. Functions and arrays may also be double precision or complex.

- Variables may be initialized by the DATA statement and subsequently changed by program statements. Variables set by a PARAMETER statement can not be changed.

EXERCISES 3.1

3.1.1. Under what restrictions on the real variables R and S, complex variable C, and integer I, are the following constructions permissible?

(a) R**I   (b) SQRT(C)   (c) C**R
(d) C**C   (e) I**R   (f) C**I

3.1.2. Insert parentheses in the following expressions such that the resulting order of operations is the same as determined by the precedence (3.1.5).

(a) A**I**J*C/D   (b) A+B/C+A/D*C

3.1.3. Give the result of the following operations if I=2 and J=3 are integers.

(a) I / J   (b) (I * J) / I
(c) I * (J I)   (d) REAL(I) / REAL(J)

3.1.4. Explain why the following Fortran construction is not valid.

```
REAL A, B
PARAMETER(A=10.0)
DATA B/10.0/
A = 100.0
B = 100.0
```

3.1.5. Write DATA statements to initialize elements of an array A declared by REAL A(10) for each of the following cases.

(a) Set A(I) = 0, for I = 1, ..., 5 and A(I) = 10.0, for I = 6, ..., 10
(b) Set A(I) = 1.0, for I = 4, ..., 8

3.2

LOGICAL VARIABLES AND DECISION STATEMENTS

In Section 2.3 we introduced the IF statement in the context of a simple decision of the form

```
IF (A.EQ.0) THEN
```

More generally, we may have

```
IF ( logical expression ) THEN
```

where *logical expression* will take on values of either true or false. The most common way of constructing logical expressions is by means of the comparison operators .EQ., .LT., and so on, shown in Table 2.3.1, and the logical operators .AND., .OR., and .NOT. For example, consider the statement

$$\text{IF((A.EQ.0) .OR. (B.LT.2.0)) PRINT*, A, B}\qquad(3.2.1)$$

If either A = 0 or B < 2 in (3.2.1), then the PRINT statement will be executed. Each of A.EQ.0 and B.LT.2.0 is itself a logical expression, taking on values true or false, and their combination with the .OR. operator gives a more complicated logical expression. We note that the inner parentheses in (3.2.1) may be removed, since the comparison operators, .EQ. and .LT., take precedence over the operator .OR.

The Logical Data Type

In conjunction with logical expressions, Fortran has a *logical data type*. Thus, the statement

$$\text{LOGICAL R, P, Q}$$

declares R, P, and Q to be *logical variables*. Logical variables take on only the values true and false, and .TRUE. and .FALSE. are the only two *logical constants*. A *logical assignment statement* is of the form, for example,

$$\text{R = (A.EQ.0) .OR. (B.LT.2.0)}\qquad(3.2.2)$$

and the logical variable R is assigned the value true or false, depending on the values of A and B. Thus, an equivalent way of writing (3.2.1) would be to follow the statement (3.2.2) by

$$\text{IF(R) PRINT*,A,B}\qquad(3.2.3)$$

Two more examples of logical expressions are

$$\text{R = (A.EQ.0) .AND. (B.LT.2.0)}\qquad(3.2.4)$$
$$\text{R = .NOT. (A.EQ.0)}\qquad(3.2.5)$$

In the first case, R takes on the value .TRUE. if and only if both A = 0 and B < 2.0 are true. The second case, (3.2.5), is equivalent to the statement

$$\text{R = A.NE.0}\qquad(3.2.6)$$

TABLE 3.2.1
Values of logical operators

Expression	Value
.NOT.P	True if P is false and false if P is true
P.AND.Q	True if and only if both P and Q are true
P.OR.Q	True if and only if either P or Q is true
P.EQV.Q	True if both P and Q are true or both are false
P.NEQV.Q	Same as .NOT.(P.EQV.Q)

so that R takes the value true if and only if $A \neq 0$. The statement (3.2.6) would be preferable to (3.2.5), although the NOT operator is sometimes very natural. Two other lesser used logical operators are .EQV. and .NEQV., denoting *equivalence* and *nonequivalence*. The values of the logical operators are summarized in Table 3.2.1, where P and Q denote logical variables or expressions. (Another way to express the content of Table 3.2.1 is given in Exercise 3.2.6.)

If we have a logical expression with two or more logical operators, for example,

$$A.GT.0 \ .OR. \ A.LT.10 \ .AND. \ B.EQ.1 \qquad (3.2.7)$$

there is a potential ambiguity: does this expression mean

$$(A.GT.0 \ .OR. \ A.LT.10) \ .AND. \ B.EQ.1 \qquad (3.2.8)$$

or

$$A.GT.0 \ .OR. \ (A.LT.10 \ .AND. \ B.EQ.1) \qquad (3.2.9)$$

They are not the same since if $B \neq 1$ and $A = 20$, (3.2.8) is false, but (3.2.9) is true. Fortran resolves this ambiguity by the precedence (left to right):

$$NOT, \ AND, \ OR, \ EQV/NEQV \qquad (3.2.10)$$

Thus, in (3.2.7), AND is performed first so that (3.2.7) is equivalent to (3.2.9). As in arithmetic expressions, parentheses override the precedence (3.2.10) so that (3.2.8) is a logical expression different than (3.2.7).

The logical operators (3.2.10) have a lower precedence then the comparison operators GT, LT, and so on. Thus, in (3.2.9), the expressions A.LT.10 and B.EQ.1 are evaluated before applying the AND operator. Similarly, the comparison operators have a lower precedence than arithmetic operators so that in

$$A.LT.B+C$$

B+C is evaluated first. However, use of parentheses is recommended in situations like this to improve readability.

In addition to logical variables, logical arrays and logical functions may also be defined. For example,

```
LOGICAL L(10)
```

declares L to be an array of 10 logical variables and

```
LOGICAL FUNCTION H(X)
```

would be the first line of a function for which the function values would be either true or false.

Nested IF statements and ELSE IF

Consider the flow chart in Figure 3.2.1. This depicts a logical flow that cannot be implemented in Fortran with a single IF statement. It can, however, be implemented by an IF statement within an IF statement, called a *nested* IF *statement*. This is illustrated in Figure 3.2.2(a). This construction can be repeated to have an IF within an IF within an IF, and so on, although deep nestings of IFs may be difficult to comprehend and should usually be avoided. However, a modification of the IF structure can sometimes make the program clearer than nested IF statements. This is illustrated in Figure 3.2.2(b), which gives an alternative implementation of the logic of Figure 3.2.1.

The general form of the ELSE IF construct is shown in Figure 3.2.3, in which arbitrarily many ELSE IF clauses are indicated. The statements following the first logical expression that is true are executed and control is then passed to the statement following END IF. If none of the logical expressions is true, the statements following the optional ELSE statement are executed. Thus, the ELSE IF construct provides a mechanism to execute

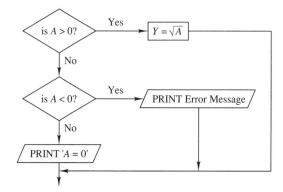

FIGURE 3.2.1
A logical flow chart

```
IF (A.GT.0) THEN
   Y= SQRT(A)                IF (A.GT.0) THEN
ELSE                            Y = SQRT(A)
   IF (A.LT.0) THEN          ELSE IF (A.LT.0) THEN
     PRINT*, 'HELP'             PRINT*, 'HELP'
   ELSE                      ELSE
     PRINT*, 'A=0'              PRINT*, 'A = 0'
   END IF                    END IF
END IF
```

   (a) Nested IF   (b) ELSE IF

FIGURE 3.2.2
Two implementations of Figure (3.2.1)

```
IF (logical expression) THEN
    statements
ELSE IF (logical expression) THEN
    .
    .
    .
ELSE IF (logical expression) THEN
    statements
ELSE
    statements
END IF
```

FIGURE 3.2.3
The general ELSE IF construction

at most one of a series of possibilities, as illustrated by Figure 3.2.2(b). Another example is given in Exercise 3.2.2.

The WHILE Statement

General logical expressions may also be used in conjunction with the WHILE construct, if this is available. The general form is

```
DO WHILE (logical expression)
    statements
END DO
```

and an example is given in Figure 3.2.4. In this example, it is assumed that A and B are real arrays of length 100. Obvious changes in both the general form and Figure 3.2.4 are necessary if your system implements the WHILE DO construction, rather than DO WHILE.

```
I = 1
DO WHILE (A(I).LT.0.AND.B(I).GT.0)
   A(I) = B(I)** 2
   I = I + 1
END DO
```

FIGURE 3.2.4
A WHILE statement

As another example, we return to the numerical integration problem of Section 2.6. We remarked there that the program of Figure 2.6.6 might not terminate if the convergence parameter ε was chosen to be too small. We can guard against this possibility by having another input parameter: the maximum number of doublings of n that will be allowed. Then the WHILE statement in Figure 2.6.6 would be modified to

$$\text{WHILE (ABS (RN-RC) .GT.EPS.AND.I.LE.IMAX) DO} \quad (3.2.11)$$

Here I is a counter that would be initialized before the WHILE statement and incremented in the body of the WHILE loop, exactly as in Figure 3.2.4. After the WHILE loop terminates, a subsequent test on the size of I would determine if convergence was achieved or not. It is left to Exercise 3.2.3 to implement these changes in the program of Figure 2.6.6.

MAIN POINTS OF SECTION 3.2

- Logical expressions may be formed by using the logical operators AND, OR, NOT, EQV, and NEQV in combination with the comparison operators EQ, GE, LE, GT, LT, and NE. IF and WHILE statements may use arbitrary logical expressions.

- Logical variables are another data type. Logical variables take on only the values TRUE or FALSE, and may be assigned the result of a logical expression.

- IF statements may be nested, but clarity is usually enhanced by using the ELSE IF construct, provided it is appropriate, rather than nested IFs.

EXERCISES 3.2

3.2.1. If I=0 and A=10.5, what is the value of the logical variable L after the following assignment statements?

(a) L = I.LE.0.OR.A.GT.12.0
(b) L = .NOT.(I.EQ.0)
(c) L = I.EQ.0.AND.A.GT.10.0.OR.A.LT.9.0

3.2.2. Give the result of the following ELSE IF construct if I = -3, I = 0, I = 21, or I=7.

```
IF (I.LT.0) THEN
   A = 0
ELSE IF (I.EQ.0) THEN
   B = 0
ELSE IF (I.GE.10) THEN
   C = 0
ELSE
   D = 0
END IF
```

3.2.3. Modify the WHILE statement in the integration program of Figure 2.6.6 so as to terminate if more than IMAX doublings of n are attempted, as discussed in the text. Add a test after the WHILE loop, and print a suitable message if convergence has not occurred.

3.2.4. If A=1, B=2, and C=3, what are the values of A, B, and C at the end of the following program segment?

```
IF (A.LE.B) THEN
   IF (C.GT.2) THEN
      C = 2
   END IF
END IF
IF (C.LT.3) THEN
   A = 0
ELSE
   B= 0
END IF
```

3.2.5. If I=0 and G=5, what are the values of I and G after the following program segment?

```
DO WHILE ((I.LE.4).AND.(G.GT.0))
   I = I + 1
   G = G - 1.0
END DO
```

3.2.6. Show that Table 3.2.1 is equivalent to the following "truth table."

P	Q	.NOT.P	P.AND.Q	P.OR.Q	P.EQV.Q	P.NEQV.Q
F	F	T	F	F	T	F
F	T	T	F	T	F	T
T	F	F	F	T	F	T
T	T	F	T	T	T	F

3.3

SCIENTIFIC COMPUTING: NONLINEAR EQUATIONS

We next consider another problem that is very important in scientific and engineering computing: the numerical solution of a nonlinear equation

$$f(x) = 0. \tag{3.3.1}$$

Some special cases of this problem are to find the roots of a polynomial

$$f(x) = a_0 + a_1 x + \cdots + a_n x^n, \tag{3.3.2}$$

or to solve transcendental equations such as

$$x - \sin x = 4. \tag{3.3.3}$$

Also, in many problems, (3.3.1) arises as the result of attempting to minimize (or maximize) a differentiable function $g(x)$. By calculus, a necessary condition for a (local) minimum is that $g'(x) = 0$; in this case, $f(x) = g'(x)$ in (3.3.1).

By the Fundamental Theorem of Algebra, a polynomial of degree n has exactly n roots, if multiple roots are counted appropriately. However, even if the coefficients $a_0, \ldots, a_n$ of the polynomial are all real, some roots may be complex; for example, the equation $x^2 + 1 = 0$ has the two solutions $\pm\sqrt{-1}$. Although in some problems it may be important to find complex solutions of (3.3.1), we will make the simplifying assumptions that x is real, $f(x)$ is real, and we wish to find only real solutions.

There are many known methods to approximate solutions of (3.3.1). We will describe two of the most basic: the *bisection method* and *Newton's method*. The bisection method is reliable, but slow, whereas Newton's method is faster, but not as reliable. After discussion of these two methods we will show how to combine them into a method that will be better than either method separately.

The Bisection Method

If f is a continuous function with $f(a) < 0$ and $f(b) > 0$, then it is intuitively clear (and can be rigorously proved) that (3.3.1) has a solution between a and b. This is illustrated in Figure 3.3.1, where $x^\star$ is the solution. Now let $x_1 = (a + b)/2$ be the midpoint of the interval (a, b). If $f(x_1) = 0$, we are done. If $f(x_1) \neq 0$ and $f(a)$ and $f(x_1)$ have different signs, then the root $x^\star$ is in the interval (a, x_1); otherwise, it is in (x_1, b). In either case, the root is now known to lie in an interval half the size of the original interval. We then repeat the process, always keeping the interval in which $x^\star$ is known to lie, and evaluating f at the midpoint of this interval in order to obtain the next interval. For example, a typical sequence of steps is shown in Figure 3.3.2 and the corresponding points x_1, x_2, and x_3 in Figure 3.3.1.

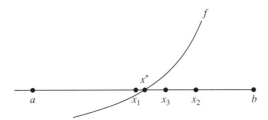

FIGURE 3.3.1
A continuous function and the bisection
method

At each step of the bisection process we obtain a new interval containing the root, and this interval is half the size of the previous interval.
Clearly, the midpoints of this sequence of intervals will converge to a root.
Thus, we may base a criterion for terminating the bisection procedure on the
following convergence test. Given a parameter ε, say $\varepsilon = 10^{-3}$, we continue
the bisection process until the current interval is of length no greater than ε.
Then we take the midpoint of this interval to be the final approximation to
the solution. This guarantees (in exact arithmetic) that the solution is correct
to $\varepsilon/2$. Thus, the parameter ε is chosen on the basis of what accuracy is
desired in the final approximation.

Figure 3.3.3 gives a Fortran program for the bisection method. The
program reads the endpoints A and B of the interval, the convergence parameter EPS, and also a maximum number of bisections to be allowed, KMAX.
The reason for KMAX will be discussed later in this section, under Errors. If
this maximum is exceeded before convergence is achieved, the message NO
CONVERGENCE is printed. The WHILE loop performs the bisection process
and prints the iteration number, the current interval A, B, the midpoint X
of this interval and the corresponding function value F (X). We note that
the FORMAT statement 10 is an example of a continued statement, the +
in column 6 indicating the continuation. The PRINT statement before the
FORMAT statement 10 is an example of a PRINT statement with no output
list; it just prints the characters shown in the FORMAT statement in order to
give headings for the table of values printed during the WHILE loop.

We now apply the bisection program to the function shown in Figure
3.3.4. This function is defined for positive values of x and has two roots, as
indicated in the figure. We are attempting to approximate the root between

$$f(x_1) < 0. \text{ Hence, } x_1 < x^* < b. \text{ Set } x_2 = \tfrac{1}{2}(x_1 + b);$$
$$f(x_2) > 0. \text{ Hence, } x_1 < x^* < x_2. \text{ Set } x_3 = \tfrac{1}{2}(x_1 + x_2);$$
$$f(x_3) > 0. \text{ Hence, } x_1 < x^* < x_3. \text{ Set } x_4 = \tfrac{1}{2}(x_1 + x_3);$$

FIGURE 3.3.2
The bisection method

```
          PROGRAM BISECT
**************************************************
* This program approximates a root between A *
* and B of a function F. It is assumed that  *
* F(A) is negative and F(B) is positive. The *
* program requires a function subprogram for *
* F, the points A and B, the convergence     *
* tolerance EPS, and the maximum number of    *
* bisections allowed, KMAX. The program       *
* prints the successive intervals and their  *
* midpoints  as the bisection proceeds.       *
**************************************************
          INTEGER K, KMAX
          REAL A, B, X, Y, EPS, F
          PRINT*, 'INPUT A, B, EPS, KMAX'
          READ*, A, B, EPS, KMAX
*  Print the input data
          PRINT 10, A, B, EPS, KMAX
 10       FORMAT('THE INPUT DATA ARE'/
     +    6X,'A=',F6.2,3X,'B=',F6.2,3X,'EPS=',
     +    F10.6,3X,'KMAX= ',I2)
*  Initialize
          K=1
          X = 0.5*(A + B)
          Y=F(X)
*  Print table headings
          PRINT 20
 20       FORMAT(/'THE RESULTS ARE'/
     +    7X,'K',6X,'X',8X,'F(X)',7X,'A',7X,'B')
*  This is the bisection loop
          DO WHILE(K.LE.KMAX.AND.(B-A).GT.EPS)
             IF (Y.LT.0) THEN
                A = X
             ELSE
                B = X
             END IF
             PRINT 30, K, X, Y, A, B
 30          FORMAT(5X,I3,2F10.6,2F9.4)
             K = K + 1
          END DO
          IF((B-A).GT.EPS) PRINT*, 'NO CONVERGENCE'
          END
*  This is the function
          REAL FUNCTION F(X)
             REAL X
             F =-1.0/X - LOG(X) + 2.0
          END
```

FIGURE 3.3.3
A bisection program

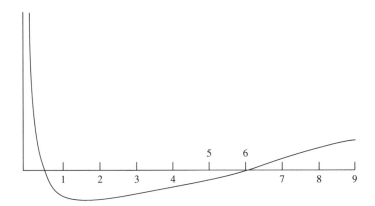

FIGURE 3.3.4
The function $f(x) = 1/x + \ell n(x) - 2$

0 and 1. The bisection method illustrated by Figures 3.3.1 and 3.3.2 is based on the assumption that $f(a) < 0$ and $f(b) > 0$. The method works just as well if $f(a) > 0$ and $f(b) < 0$, but the decisions must be reversed from those in Figure 3.3.2. For example, if $f(x_1) < 0$, then $a < x^* < x_1$, and so on (see Exercise 3.3.1). Alternatively, when $f(a) > 0 > f(b)$, we may work with $-f(x)$ and use the original algorithm. This is what we have done for the function of Figure 3.3.4, using its negative in the function subprogram in Figure 3.3.2.

Figure 3.3.5 gives sample output for the data A=0, B=1, EPS=0.01, KMAX=8. Note that the function is not defined for 0, but this is an acceptable value since the bisection method will never evaluate the function at the endpoints of the interval. The sample output shows that the intervals are converging to the root, whose value is 0.3178. After seven bisections, we have approximated this root to almost three decimal places. If the parameter

```
THE INPUT DATA ARE
A=  0.00    B=  1.00     EPS=  0.010000     KMAX=  8

THE RESULTS ARE
K       X            F(X)        A         B
1   0.250000  -0.613706    0.0000    0.5000
2   0.375000   0.314162    0.2500    0.5000
3   0.312500  -0.036849    0.2500    0.3750
4   0.343750   0.158750    0.3125    0.3750
5   0.328125   0.066741    0.3125    0.3438
6   0.320313   0.016507    0.3125    0.3281
7   0.316406  -0.009766    0.3125    0.3203
```

FIGURE 3.3.5
Output from bisection program: root = 0.31784443

EPS were smaller and KMAX larger, still more accuracy would be obtained after further bisections (Exercise 3.3.2).

Newton's Method

The bisection method is simple and reliable, but is rather slow. A potentially much faster method may be derived as follows. Let x_0 be an approximation to the solution x^*, and draw the tangent line to the curve of f at x_0, as shown in Figure 3.3.6. Then, take the intersection of this tangent line with the x-axis as a new approximation to x^*.

We now need to formulate this geometric procedure analytically so that we may compute the new approximation x_1. The tangent function is

$$T(x) \equiv f'(x_0)(x - x_0) + f(x_0).$$

The next approximation, x_1, is then the solution of the equation

$$T(x) = 0,$$

which gives

$$x_1 = x_0 - \frac{f(x_0)}{f'(x_0)}.$$

We may now repeat this process, replacing x_0 by x_1 to obtain another approximation, and then repeat again, and so on. Thus, we can generate a sequence of approximations by

$$x_{k+1} = x_k - \frac{f(x_k)}{f'(x_k)}, \quad k = 0, 1, \ldots \tag{3.3.4}$$

This is *Newton's Method* for approximating a solution of a nonlinear equation.

We next discuss some properties of Newton's method. First, it is clear that $f'(x_k)$ must be nonzero to avoid division by zero in (3.3.4). Geometrically, if $f'(x_k) = 0$, the tangent line at x_k is horizontal, and thus has no

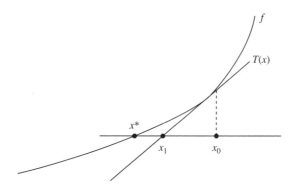

FIGURE 3.3.6
Newton's Method

intersection with the x-axis. Assuming that we avoid division by zero, the two main properties of Newton's method are:

Convergence

If x_0 is sufficiently close to $x^\star$, then $x_k \to x^\star$ as $k \to \infty$.   (3.3.5)

Quadratic Convergence

If f is twice continuously differentiable, if $f'(x^\star) \neq 0$, and if $x_k \to x^\star$ as $k \to \infty$, then

$$|x_{k+1} - x^\star| \doteq c|x_k - x^\star|^2 \text{ as } k \to \infty \qquad (3.3.6)$$

where c is some constant. The second property of *quadratic convergence* ensures that once the iterates get close to the solution, they converge very rapidly, approximately doubling the number of correct digits each iteration.

As an illustration of quadratic convergence in Newton's method, we again consider the function of Figure 3.3.4. Table 3.3.1 contains a summary of the first six iterations of Newton's method using the starting value $x_0 = 0.1$; the root is obtained to eight decimal places in six Newton iterations. Note that once an approximation is "close enough" (in this case, after three iterations), the number of correct digits doubles in each iteration, showing the quadratic convergence.

In order to stop the Newton iteration we will use the convergence test

$$|f(x_k)| \leq \varepsilon \qquad (3.3.7)$$

where ε is a small number, say 10^{-4} or 10^{-6}. The criterion (3.3.7) does not guarantee that x_k is close to $x^\star$, but it does say that we have found an approximate solution in the sense that $f(x_k)$ is small.

We next give a pseudocode for Newton's method in Figure 3.3.7, using the convergence test (3.3.7), as well as a maximum allowed number of iterations. In this pseudocode, a `WHILE` statement terminates the Newton iteration if there is convergence, or if $f'(x_i) = 0$, or if a prescribed maximum number of iterations has been exceeded. Subsequent tests are then required to ascertain which of these conditions occurred. It is left to Exercise 3.3.3 to write a Fortran program for Newton's method, following the pseudocode of Figure 3.3.7.

TABLE 3.3.1
Convergence of Newton's Method to Root = 0.31784443

Iteration	x_{i-1}	$f(x_{i-1})$	x_i	Number of Correct Digits
1	0.1	5.6974149	0.16330461	0
2	0.16330461	2.3113878	0.23697659	0
3	0.23697659	0.7800322	0.29438633	1
4	0.29438633	0.1740346	0.31576121	2
5	0.31576121	0.0141811	0.31782764	4
6	0.31782764	0.0001134	0.31784443	8

Input: $x_0, \varepsilon, \max i, f, f'$
Set $i = 0$
While ($i \leq \max i$ and $|f(x_i)| > \varepsilon$ and $f'(x_i) \neq 0$)
    $x_{i+1} = x_i - f(x_i)/f'(x_i)$
    $i = i + 1$
End While
If $f'(x_i) = 0$, output error message
Else if $i > \max i$, output message
Else output x_i as solution

FIGURE 3.3.7
A pseudocode for Newton's method

Errors

Iterative methods such as the bisection method or Newton's method are subject to error that is somewhat akin to discretization error. In an iterative process, a sequence of approximations to a solution is generated with the hope that the approximations will converge to the solution; in many cases mathematical proofs can be given that show convergence will occur as the number of iterations tends to infinity. However, only a finite number of such approximations can ever be generated on a computer, and, therefore, we must necessarily stop short of mathematical convergence. The error caused by such finite termination of an iterative process is sometimes called *convergence error*, although there is no generally accepted terminology here.

There is another aspect of convergence error when rounding error is present. Consider Newton's method. When the iterates x_k approach the solution x^*, $f(x_k)$ becomes small and the sign of $f(x_k)$ may be evaluated incorrectly. If the sign of $f'(x_k)$ is correct, which will be true if $f'(x_k)$ is not small, then the change in the iterate, $f(x_k)/f'(x_k)$, has the wrong sign and the computed next iterate moves in the wrong direction. The same difficulty may occur in the bisection method; if the sign of $f(x_k)$ is incorrect, a wrong decision will be made as to the next interval to retain. Because of this, with both of these methods as well as others, there will tend to be an erratic behavior of the iterates when errors in the sign of $f(x_k)$ occur, and then it is no longer useful to continue the iteration. This is one reason that only a maximum number of iterations should be allowed, since convergence may never occur if the convergence parameter is too small.

With the bisection method without rounding error, convergence is guaranteed once we have a suitable starting interval. With Newton's method the situation is different. The convergence property (3.3.5) of Newton's method stated that if x_0 is sufficiently close to the solution x^*, the Newton iterates will converge to x^*. Convergence will also occur if any iterate x_k gets sufficiently close to x^*; otherwise, various types of bad behavior may occur. For example, $f'(x_k)$ may be zero and the iteration stops. Or, as illustrated in Figure 3.3.8, successive iterations diverge from x^*.

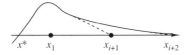

FIGURE 3.3.8
Divergence of Newton iterates

A Combined Newton-Bisection Method

In order to mitigate these problems with Newton's method, we will combine it with the bisection method, as indicated by the flow chart in Figure 3.3.9. In this figure, we assume that we start with x_0 in an interval (a, b), for which $f(a) < 0 < f(b)$. If $f'(x_0) = 0$, or if the next Newton iterate is outside the current interval (a, b), we perform a bisection step to obtain a smaller interval, also denoted by (a, b), and then try the Newton process again. Thus, the Newton iterates can not "escape"; they either converge or we obtain a shrinking set of intervals by bisection. As with the Newton method itself, we should add to the flow chart a test that will cause termination if a maximum number of iterations is exceeded. Exercise 3.3.5 requests that you write a Fortran program to implement the flow chart of Figure 3.3.9.

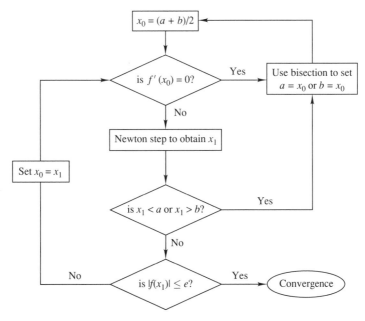

FIGURE 3.3.9
Combined Newton-Bisection method: $f(a) < 0 < f(b)$

There are many possible variations on Figure 3.3.9. For example, after a successful Newton step we could use the Newton iterate x_1 as one endpoint of a new interval in which the root lies. This would prevent another possible difficulty with Newton's method, known as *cycling*, in which we can have $x_2 = x_0$ so that no convergence is obtained, even though the iterates do not diverge.

MAIN POINTS OF SECTION 3.3

- Two simple methods for approximating solutions of an equation $f(x) = 0$ are the bisection method and Newton's method.

- The bisection method is reliable, but slow. Newton's method is potentially much faster (quadratic convergence), but may not converge. A combination of the two methods ensures reliability.

- Both the bisection method and Newton's method may be affected by rounding error if the sign of the function is not evaluated correctly.

EXERCISES 3.3

3.3.1. Redo the program of Figure 3.3.3 so that the bisection algorithm works for the case that $f(a) > 0$ and $f(b) < 0$.

3.3.2. Run the program of Figure 3.3.3 for different values of EPS and KMAX. How many bisections do you need to take in order to approximate the root to 6 decimal places?

3.3.3. Write a Fortran program for Newton's method, following the pseudocode of Figure 3.3.7. Run the program for the function of Figure 3.3.4 and see if you can reproduce the results of Table 3.3.1.

3.3.4. Let $f(x) = x - \sin x$. This function has three roots: 0 and one in each of the intervals $(\pi/2, 2)$ and $(-2, -\pi/2)$. Attempt to find the positive root by both the bisection method and Newton's method, using the programs of Figure 3.3.3 and Exercise 3.3.3. Experiment with different starting values for Newton's method within the interval $(\pi/2, 2)$. Graph the function and try to ascertain geometrically what starting values will give convergence.

3.3.5. Write a Fortran program for a combined Newton-bisection method along the lines of Figure 3.3.9, with the loop implemented by a WHILE construct. Add a test to terminate on a given maximum number of iterations if convergence has not occurred. Run your program on the equation of Exercise 3.3.4 using some initial x_0 for which Newton's method didn't converge.

3.4

MORE ON DO LOOPS AND ARRAYS

We have so far used only basic DO loops of the form

```
DO 10 I = 1, N
     statements
 10 CONTINUE
```
(3.4.1)

However, much more general control of the loop is possible. For example, the loop variable I in (3.4.1) takes the values $1, 2, 3, \ldots, N$, but we can use only a subset of these by the construction

```
DO 10 I = 1, N, 2
```
(3.4.2)

The parameter 2 in (3.4.2) is called the *step* or *stride*, and the effect is that I will now take on only the values $I = 1, 3, 5, \ldots$. Also, the starting value of I does not need to be 1; for example, in the statement

```
DO 10 I = 2, 20, 2
```
(3.4.3)

I will take on the values $2, 4, 6, \ldots, 20$. When using a step not equal to 1, caution is required to ensure that the loop terminates with the desired value of I. For example, in the statement

```
DO 10 I = 1,20,2
```

the last value of I will be 19, not 21. The general rule is that the last value of I will be less then or equal to the maximum value specified in the loop. The value of the step can be any integer, not just 2. For example,

```
DO 10 I = 1, N, 5
```

will use the values $I = 1, 6, 11, \ldots$. The step may also be negative, as in

```
DO 10 I = 10, 1, -1
```

Here, the values of I are $10, 9, 8, \ldots, 1$, in that order, so that the loop runs "backwards". In general, the control statement of a DO loop has the form

```
DO 10 I =  first, last, step
```
(3.4.4)

where *first, last,* and *step* can be expressions. For example, in the statement

```
DO 10 I = J + K, N * N, J * K
```

each of the expressions would be evaluated using the current values of the integers J, K, and N, in order to set the parameters of the DO loop before execution. However, it is not wise to use complicated expressions in this context, since the program may be more difficult to understand.

The use of expressions in (3.4.4) leads to the possibility that the loop will not execute at all, which may be what is desired. For example, in

```
DO 50 I = K, 10
```

if the current value of K is greater than 10, the DO loop will be bypassed. (In older versions of Fortran, the loop would automatically be executed once, sometimes leading to interesting results.)

Fortran also allows the values of *first, last*, and *step* in (3.4.4) to be real variables. For example, the statement

```
DO 10 X = 0.1, 1.0, 0.1                              (3.4.5)
```

where X is a real variable, is permissible. However, it is extremely dangerous to use a real variable as the loop index since numbers like 0.1 do not have an exact binary representation. This, combined with rounding error, may cause the loop not to perform the expected number of times. Consequently, real variables to control a DO loop should never be used. The effect of (3.4.5) can be achieved by

```
DO 10 I = 1,10
X = 0.1*REAL(I)
```

Another bad DO loop practice is the attempt to change the parameters within the loop. For example, within the body of a DO loop begun by

```
DO 10 I = 1, N
```

a statement of the form I = I + 1 that tried to change the loop variable I would result in an error message on compilation. A statement of the form N = 2*N within the body would be legal, and does not change the number of times the loop is repeated. However, this is bad practice and should be avoided. Also, the value of the loop parameter I is local to the DO loop, and it is dangerous to assume its value outside the loop. For example, consider the statements

```
DO 10 I = 1, 5
   ⋮
10 CONTINUE
J = I * I
```

You might expect that the value of I used in the statement following 10 is 6, but you should assume that it is undefined and never use such a construction.

Arrays

In Chapter 2, we saw that real or integer arrays could be defined by declarations such as

```
REAL A(100)
INTEGER S(20)
```

These declarations define arrays with elements $A(1), A(2), \ldots, A(100)$ and $S(1), \ldots, S(20)$. However, we can also define arrays whose indices have a different range, including negative values. For example, the statement

```
REAL A(0:10), B(-10:10), C(10:20)
```

defines an array A with 11 elements $A(0), A(1), \ldots, A(10)$, an array B with 21 elements $B(-10), B(-9), \ldots, B(10)$, and an array C with 11 elements $C(10), C(11), \ldots, C(20)$. Any reference to an array element outside the defined range is illegal; for example, we cannot reference $C(1)$ since this is undefined. In general, the form of the declaration is

$$\text{REAL A } (i_1 : i_2) \tag{3.4.6}$$

where i_1 and i_2 are any positive or negative integers satisfying $i_1 \leq i_2$. The same construction may be used to define integer, complex, double precision or logical arrays.

In general, i_1 and i_2 must be integer constants in (3.4.6). Integer variables are not allowed except for arrays declared within subprograms, or if the variables are declared by a parameter statement. For example,

```
PARAMETER(M = 100)
REAL A(0:M), B(M)
```

is permissible. Indeed, it is advisable to use this construction when the size of an array may change for different uses of the program.

Previously, we have indexed array elements only by, say, $A(3)$ or $A(I)$, but we can use any integer expression as the index, for example

```
A(I + 1), A(I * J), A((I * I) + (J ** 5))
```

Generally, it is not good practice to use complicated expressions as array indices. Integer-valued array elements or functions may also be used as indices; for example, $A(K(I))$ is permitted, where K is either an array or function. In this context, K is sometimes called a *pointer* array or function. The important concept of pointers will be discussed further in Chapter 4 as part of Fortran 90.

Evaluating Polynomials

We now give some examples of the constructs just discussed. Suppose that we wish to apply Newton's method, discussed in Section 3.3, to a polynomial equation $p(x) = 0$, where

$$p(x) = a_0 + a_1 x + \cdots + a_n x^n. \qquad (3.4.7)$$

Each iteration of Newton's method requires the evaluation of p and p' at the current iterate, where

$$p'(x) = a_1 + 2a_2 x + 3a_3 x^2 + \cdots + n a_n x^{n-1}. \qquad (3.4.8)$$

Consider the evaluation of $p(x)$ for some particular value x. A straightforward approach is to compute $x^2, x^3, \ldots, x^n$, and then perform a dot product (Section 2.4) of the two vectors

$$(a_0, a_1, \ldots, a_n) \quad (1, x, x^2, \ldots, x^n). \qquad (3.4.9)$$

This requires n multiplications and n additions plus forming the powers of x. A more efficient technique is *Horner's rule*, also called the *nested form*, which for $n = 3$ is

$$p(x) = ((a_3 x + a_2)x + a_1)x + a_0. \qquad (3.4.10)$$

Here, $a_3 x + a_2$ is evaluated first, then multiplied by x, and so on. In general,

$$p(x) = (\cdots ((a_n x + a_{n-1})x + a_{n-2})x + \cdots + a_1)x + a_0. \qquad (3.4.11)$$

The evaluation of p by (3.4.11) requires n multiplications and n additions (check this for (3.4.10)), the same as the dot product of the vectors of (3.4.9), but avoids the extra computation of the powers of x. Usually it also has less rounding error.

A function subprogram for the evaluation of $p(x)$ by (3.4.11) is given in Figure 3.4.1. This function illustrates using an array starting with index 0, which is very natural for the coefficients $a_0, \ldots, a_n$. It also illustrates a backward DO loop, which is also very natural for the computation (3.4.11).

The same function may be used to evaluate the derivative in (3.4.8), but first we need to compute the coefficients of p'. Figure 3.4.2 gives a

```
FUNCTION F(X,A,N)
    INTEGER N,J
    REAL F, X, A(0:N)
    F = A(N)
    DO 10 J = N-1, 0, -1
        F = (F * X) + A(J)
10      CONTINUE
    END
```

FIGURE 3.4.1

Polynomial evaluation by Horner's rule

```
        SUBROUTINE DIF(A,N,D)
           INTEGER N,I
           REAL A(0:N),  D(0:N)
           DO 10 I = 1, N
              D(I-1) =  REAL (I) * A(I)
10         CONTINUE
           END
```

FIGURE 3.4.2
Obtaining the derivative

subroutine that accepts the array A of coefficients of p and returns an array D of coefficients of the derivative. This is a very simple example of a *symbolic differentiation* program, in which the input represents a function and the output represents its derivative. (There are a number of programs, such as Mathematica, Macsyma, and Maple, designed to perform symbolic computations.)

In a program for Newton's method, the function F of Figure 3.4.1 may be called for evaluating p, the subroutine of Figure 3.4.2 called for obtaining the array of coefficients of p', and then F again called by F(X,D,N-1) to evaluate p'. This could all be combined into one subroutine, of course, if desired (see Exercise 3.4.4).

MAIN POINTS OF SECTION 3.4

- The general form of the control statement of a DO loop is

  DO statement number I = first, last, step

  where *first, last,* and *step* are arbitrary integer expressions. Although *first, last,* and *step* may also be real, this capability should never be used.

- Arrays may be declared by TYPE $A(i_1 : i_2)$, where i_1 and i_2 are (possibly negative) integers with $i_1 \leq i_2$. Here TYPE may be real, integer, double precision, complex or logical. The array elements A(I) are defined only for $i_1 \leq I \leq i_2$. i_1 and i_2 may be variables if they have been set previously by a PARAMETER statement.

- Polynomials may be evaluated efficiently by Horner's rule.

EXERCISES 3.4

3.4.1. Suppose that A is an array of real numbers satisfying $A(I+1) \leq A(I)$ for $I = 0, \ldots, 99$. Declare A and write a program segment using WHILE to determine how many elements of the array A are ≥ 0.1.

3.4.2. If A is an integer array with the values $A(I) = I, I = 1, \ldots, 6$, before the following DO loop, give the values of the array after the loop terminates.

```
DO 10 I = 6, 1, -2
   A(I) = A(I) + 1
10 CONTINUE
```

3.4.3. Assume that A and B are arrays declared by

```
REAL A(30), B(10)
```

Write a DO loop that will assign to A every third element of A.

3.4.4. Combine the programs of Figures 3.4.1 and 3.4.2 into a single subroutine that accepts the coefficients of a polynomial p and an argument x and outputs the values of $p(x)$ and $p'(x)$. Write a main program that will call this subroutine. Test it for the polynomial

$$p(x) = 1.0 + 3.5x + 4.1x^2 + 32.0x^3$$

3.5

TWO-DIMENSIONAL ARRAYS

Much of scientific and engineering computation involves vectors and matrices. A vector is represented in a natural way in Fortran by the arrays we have discussed. For example, the vector with real elements

$$\mathbf{x} = \begin{bmatrix} x_1 \\ \vdots \\ x_{10} \end{bmatrix}$$

would be declared by

```
REAL X(10)
```

A *matrix* A is an $m \times n$ array of the form

$$A = \begin{bmatrix} a_{11} & \cdots & a_{1n} \\ \vdots & & \\ a_{m1} & \cdots & a_{mn} \end{bmatrix}$$

with m rows and n columns. Two examples are

$$A = \begin{bmatrix} 2 & 1 & 2 \\ 3 & 2 & 4 \end{bmatrix} \qquad A = \begin{bmatrix} 1 & 1 & 2 \\ 4 & 2 & 1 \\ 6 & 4 & 2 \end{bmatrix}$$

with $m = 2$ and $n = 3$ in the first case, and $m = n = 3$ in the second. Matrices may be represented in Fortran by *two-dimensional arrays*, defined by a declaration such as

    REAL A(8,10)

This declares A to be an array with 8 rows and 10 columns so that it represents a 8×10 matrix. Integer arrays may be declared in a similar way: the statement

    INTEGER S(4,2)

defines S to be a 4×2 array of integers. Two-dimensional complex, double precision and logical arrays may also be declared.

Just as with one-dimensional arrays, the index range of two-dimensional arrays may be specified. For example, the declaration

    REAL A(0:9,-5:5)   (3.5.1)

defines an 10×11 two-dimensional array with elements

$$A(I, J), \quad I = 0, \ldots, 9, \quad J = -5, -4, \ldots, 5.$$

The general form is

    REAL A($i_1 : i_2$, $j_1 : j_2$)

where i_1, i_2, j_1, j_2 are any positive or negative integers satisfying $i_1 \le i_2$ and $j_1 \le j_2$. These integers may also be specified by a PARAMETER statement.

Higher-dimensional Arrays

We can also declare arrays of more than two dimensions. For example,

    REAL B(10,10,10)   (3.5.2)

defines a three-dimensional array of $10 \times 10 \times 10 = 1000$ elements. In general, Fortran allows arrays of up to seven dimensions, although more than three dimensions are rarely used.

The *rank* of an array is the number of dimensions; the *extent* along a dimension is the length of the array in that dimension. The *size* of an array is the total number of elements in the array and is the product of the extents in each dimension. The *shape* of an array is the sequence of extents. For example, the size of the array A of (3.5.1) is 110 and its shape is (10,11), indicating 10 elements in the first dimension and 11 in the second dimension. Two arrays are *conformable* if they have the same shape. For example, the array (3.5.1) is conformable with the array declared by

    REAL C(10,11)

since both have 10 rows and 11 columns.

B(1, 1)	B(1, 2)	B(1, 3)
B(2, 1)	B(2, 2)	B(2, 3)
B(3, 1)	B(3, 2)	B(3, 3)

first column	second column	third column
B(1, 1), B(2, 1), B(3, 1),	B(1, 2), B(2, 2), B(3, 2),	B(1, 3), B(2, 3), B(3, 3)

FIGURE 3.5.1
Storage of two-dimensional array

Initialization of Arrays

Two- and higher-dimensional arrays may be initialized by the DATA statement. For example, if B is declared by (3.5.2), the statement

```
DATA B/1000*0/
```

will set all elements of B to zero. Implied DO loops may also be used; if A is declared by (3.5.1) the statement

```
DATA ((A(I,J), I=0,9),J=1,5)/50*1.0/
```

will initialize the indicated elements of A to 1.0. Note that the number of elements between //, 50 in this example, must match exactly the number of elements called for in the implied DO loop, or a compiler error will occur.

Storage of Arrays

For many purposes, it is important to know how arrays are stored in memory. For one-dimensional arrays there is no problem: for the array A declared by

```
REAL A(10), B(3,3)
```

10 consecutive memory locations are reserved for A. For two-dimensional arrays, however, there are different possibilities. In Fortran, storage is *column-major*[1]; that is, if we view B as a matrix, the first column is stored, followed by the second column, and so on, as illustrated in Figure 3.5.1. In this figure, the elements of B are shown in matrix form, and then as a linear sequence in the order in which they appear in memory.

---

[1]The Fortran 90 standard, however, does not specify how arrays are stored.

Higher-dimensional arrays are stored in an analogous way: the first index varies most rapidly, followed by the second index, and so on. For example, if A is declared by REAL A(2,2,2), the elements of A would be stored in the order

A(1,1,1) A(2,1,1) A(1,2,1) A(2,2,1) A(1,1,2) A(2,1,2) A(1,2,2) A(2,2,2)

Other programming languages may use a *row-major* convention, in which a two-dimensional array is stored by rows rather than columns.

Arrays as Subprogram Arguments

We have previously used one-dimensional arrays as arguments of sub-programs, and the same can be done with arrays of any dimension. We will illustrate this by one of the most basic operations in matrix algebra: multiplication of a vector by a matrix. If A is an $n \times n$ matrix and $\mathbf{x}$ is an n long vector, the *matrix-vector product* $A\mathbf{x}$ is an n long vector $\mathbf{b}$, whose components are defined by

$$b_i = \sum_{j=1}^{n} a_{ij} x_j, \quad i = 1, \ldots, n. \qquad (3.5.3)$$

Figure 3.5.2 gives a subroutine for doing this matrix-vector multiplication.

The program in Figure 3.5.2 gives an example of a *nested* DO *loop*, in which a DO loop appears within another DO loop. Such nesting of DO loops is common in matrix computations. Note that the statement B(I)=0 ensures that this component of B is zero before the beginning of the following DO loop; if the initial value of B(I) were not zero, the final result would be in error.

The subroutine of Figure 3.5.2 may be called for arrays of different sizes; for example, in the main program we might have the statements

```
        SUBROUTINE MATVEC(A,X,B,N)
        INTEGER I, J, N
        REAL A(N,N), X(N), B(N)
        DO 20 I = 1,N
          B(I) = 0
          DO 10 J = 1,N
            B(I) = B(I) + A(I,J) * X(J)
10        CONTINUE
20      CONTINUE
        END
```

FIGURE 3.5.2
Subroutine for matrix-vector multiplication

```
REAL B(3,3), Z(3), U(3), C(20,20), Q(20), V(20)
CALL MATVEC (B, Z, U, 3)
CALL MATVEC (C, Q, V, 20)
```

Printing and Reading Two-dimensional Arrays

There are a number of ways to print two-dimensional arrays. For example, if P is a 4×4 array, the statements shown in Figure 3.5.3(a) will display the elements of the array P, one per line.

On the other hand, the statements in Figure 3.5.3(b) will display P a row per line. Here, the format statement could have used 4F6.2, but the outcome is the same with 6F6.2 since P has only four elements per row. Still another possibility is the doubly implied DO loop

```
PRINT 100, ((P(I,J), J = 1,4), I = 1,4)        (3.5.4)
```

However, if 100 is still the format statement in Figure 3.5.3(b), (3.5.4) will display six entries per line, not just a row of four entries. The reason is that now the whole array of 16 elements is considered the variable list to be displayed, and the format statement determines how many elements are printed per line. This is in contrast to the construction of Figure 3.5.3(b), in which four PRINT statements are initiated, each printing a new line.

We can also use just the array identifier to print the whole array:

```
PRINT 100, P                                   (3.5.5)
```

This is not equivalent to (3.5.4), however, since the elements of P will be displayed in the order they appear in storage, namely, by column. Another

```
      DO 30 I = 1,4
        DO 20 J=1,4
          PRINT*, P(I,J)
20      CONTINUE
30      CONTINUE
```

(a) One per line

```
      DO 30 I = 1, 4
        PRINT 100, (P(I,J),J=1,4)
100   FORMAT (6F6.2)
 30   CONTINUE
```

(b) Four per line

FIGURE 3.5.3
Printing array elements

caution with (3.5.5) is the following. Suppose that P has been declared as a 10×10 array but only elements in the first 4×4 subarray have been assigned values. Then (3.5.4) will print only these values, but (3.5.5) will attempt to print the whole 10×10 array. On some systems (for example, WATFOR) those elements of the array that have not been assigned values will be printed as ????, or some other error indication. However, other systems may halt with a run-time error.

All of the above constructions may also be used with the WRITE statement. For example, (3.5.5) could be written as

```
WRITE (7,100) P
```
(3.5.6)

if we wished to write P to a file identified by an OPEN statement. They may also be used with the READ statement, and have essentially the same restrictions. For example, if PRINT* in Figure 3.5.3(a) is replaced by READ*, sixteen read operations will be initiated, each requiring one input from the keyboard. Similarly, the statements

```
      DO 10 I = 1, 4
         READ*, (P(I,J), J=1,4)
10       CONTINUE
```

will initiate four read operations, each expecting four inputs from the keyboard, and

```
READ*, ((P(I,J), J = 1,4), I = 1,4)
```
(3.5.7)

will initiate a single read operation that requires sixteen inputs. Analogous to (3.5.7) we may also write

```
READ* , P
```
(3.5.8)

which will again require 16 inputs. The difference between (3.5.7) and (3.5.8) is the same as for printing: (3.5.7) will store the inputs in the row-order P(1,1), P(1,2), P(1,3), ..., whereas (3.5.8) will store them in the column-order P(1,1), P(2,1), P(3,1), ... A statement such as (3.5.7) explicitly gives the order in which the inputs are to be stored but (3.5.8) will use the column-major order.

Inefficiencies in Arrays

Although two- and higher-dimensional arrays are very useful, there are some inefficiences associated with their use, and the programmer should be aware of these. Many matrices in applications have mostly zero elements.

An important example is a *tridiagonal* matrix.

$$\begin{bmatrix} a_{11} & a_{12} & & & \\ a_{21} & a_{22} & a_{23} & & \\ & a_{32} & \ddots & \ddots & \\ & & \ddots & \ddots & a_{n-1,n} \\ & & & a_{n,n-1} & a_{nn} \end{bmatrix} \qquad (3.5.9)$$

in which all elements are zero, except those on the main diagonal and the two adjacent diagonals. If this matrix is stored in an $n \times n$ two-dimensional array, then n^2 storage locations will be reserved, even though only $3n - 2$ are required. Such matrices are usually stored in three one-dimensional arrays, one for each diagonal.

Another source of inefficiency is in accessing the elements of two- (and higher) dimensional arrays. Suppose that we have the declaration

        REAL A(100,50), B(100)   (3.5.10)

and the statement

        Y = A(I,J)

which requires addressing the Ith element in the Jth column of A. Since two-dimensional arrays are stored in memory one column after another, the compiler will set up code to compute the address of A(I,J) as

        BASE + 100 * (J-1) + I   (3.5.11)

Here BASE is the memory address minus one of the first element of the array and 100 is the number of rows in the array, as given by (3.5.10). Thus, (3.5.11) must be evaluated for the current values of I and J in order to give the location in memory of the (I,J) element of the array. However, for the statement

        Z = B(I)

where B is defined by (3.5.10), the corresponding calculation for the memory address is

        BASE + I

which requires only an addition. Thus, memory addresses of two-dimensional arrays are more expensive to compute since they require a multiplication and three additions (including subtractions), as opposed to a single addition. (However, if the address of A(I,J) has been computed, the address of A(I+1,J) may be obtained by adding 1, and the address of A(I,J+1) obtained by adding the number of rows in the array. Many compilers will compute subsequent addresses in this more efficient way.)

The above discussion is not meant to imply that two-dimensional arrays should not be used, but only to indicate that their use may be more expensive than one-dimensional arrays. If there is no good reason to use two-dimensional arrays, they should be avoided. For example, another way to store the tridiagonal matrix (3.5.9) is by a two-dimensional $n \times 3$ array in which each column of the array is a diagonal of the matrix. Thus, only $3n$ storage locations are reserved, but access to the elements must use a two-dimensional mechanism such as (3.5.11). As mentioned previously, it is usually preferable to store this matrix in three one-dimensional arrays.

MAIN POINTS OF SECTION 3.5

- Two-dimensional arrays are a natural way to represent matrices. The declaration TYPE A($i_1 : i_2; j_1 : j_2$) defines a two-dimensional array with subscript ranges $i_1 \leq$ I $\leq i_2$ and $j_1 \leq$ J$\leq j_2$, and where TYPE may be REAL, INTEGER, COMPLEX, DOUBLE PRECISION, or LOGICAL. Arrays of up to seven dimensions may be declared.

- Arrays are stored by the column-major convention. In particular, two-dimensional arrays are stored one column after another.

- Two-dimensional arrays may be printed and read in a number of different ways, using explicit or implied DO loops, or just the array name itself. In the latter case, the printing (reading) order follows the column-major storage convention.

- Use of two-dimensional arrays can give rise to inefficiencies in both storage and array element access.

EXERCISES 3.5

3.5.1. Program the subroutine of Figure 3.5.2 and test it for various matrices A and vectors $\mathbf{x}$ of size $N = 2$ and $N = 3$.

3.5.2. The sum $C = A + B$ of two $N \times M$ matrices A and B is defined by

$$c_{ij} = a_{ij} + b_{ij}, \quad i = 1, \ldots, N, \quad j = 1, \ldots, M.$$

Write a subroutine that accepts A, B, N, M as inputs and computes C as an output array.

3.5.3. The *Schur product* C of two $N \times M$ matrices A and B is defined by

$$c_{ij} = a_{ij}b_{ij}, \quad i = 1, \ldots, N, \quad j = 1, \ldots, M.$$

Write a subroutine that accepts A, B, N, M as inputs and computes as outputs C and the sum of the absolute values of the elements of C.

3.5.4. The product of two $n \times n$ matrices A and B is an $n \times n$ matrix C whose i, j element is

$$c_{ij} = \sum_{k=1}^{n} a_{ik} b_{kj}.$$

Write a subroutine that accepts n, A, and B as inputs and outputs the product matrix C.

3.5.5. Give a declaration statement for a real two-dimensional array A and a single READ statement so that at the end of the READ, A will have values in positions $A(\pm I, \pm J)$, for $I, J = 0, \ldots, 5$.

3.6

MORE ON SUBPROGRAMS

Functions as Subprogram Arguments

Suppose that we have a subroutine that utilizes values of a function F. For example, within the body of the subroutine there may be a statement such as

```
X = F(Y) + 4.0
```
(3.6.1)

However, we may wish to perform the computation (3.6.1) for different functions on different calls of the subroutine. In this case, we would like the function to be an argument of the subroutine. We can achieve this by a subroutine heading such as

```
SUBROUTINE SUB(A,B,F)
```

in which the function F is included in the argument list of the subroutine. Then, the subroutine may be called with different functions, for example

```
CALL SUB(X,Y,G)
```
(3.6.2)
```
CALL SUB(Z,W,H)
```
(3.6.3)

where G and H are functions that will replace F in the statement (3.6.1). It is necessary to declare the functions appearing in CALL statements like those of (3.6.2) and (3.6.3) to be *external* by the statement

```
EXTERNAL G,H
```

which would be at the beginning of the main program. This is illustrated by the schematic of Figure 3.6.1, where the first call of the subroutine uses the function R in place of F, and the second call uses the function Q.

Functions may also be arguments of functions, as well as subroutines, by using exactly the same construction. For example, in the definition

```
REAL FUNCTION CAN(X,G)
```

G may be a function. Then in the main program CAN might be called by

$$Y = CAN(2.0, G1) **4 \qquad (3.6.4)$$

where G1 is the actual function used and will appear in an **EXTERNAL** statement. We caution that statement functions may not be used as subprogram arguments.

Intrinsic functions may also be used as arguments. For example, in place of (3.6.4) we may have the statements

```
Y = CAN(2.0, SIN)
```

or

```
Y = CAN(2.0, COS)
```

in the main program, where **SIN** and **COS** are the intrinsic functions for sine and cosine. In this case, in place of the **EXTERNAL** statement, we would use the statement

```
INTRINSIC SIN, COS
```

indicating that **SIN** and **COS** are intrinsic functions.

```
PROGRAM MAIN                    SUBROUTINE SUB(A,B,F)
REAL A,B                            (Statements)
EXTERNAL R, Q                   Y = F(Y) + 4.0
     (Statements)                   (Statements)
CALL SUB(A,B,R)                 END
     (Statements)              REAL FUNCTION R(W)
CALL SUB(A,B,Q)                     (Statements)
     (Statements)              END
END                            REAL FUNCTION Q(Z)
                                    (Statements)
                               END
```

FIGURE 3.6.1
Functions as arguments

A warning is in order at this point. Some intrinsic functions are called *generic* and their type does not need to be declared. For example, the function ABS is a generic function and its argument may be either real or integer, the function value taking the type of the argument. However, there is also an intrinsic function named IABS, which assumes integer arguments and returns an integer function value. If you use ABS as a function argument it is assumed to be a real function; if you wish the integer function you must use IABS. In general, specific names, such as IABS, of generic intrinsic functions must be used as subprogram arguments. These specific names are given in Appendix 2.

Saving Local Variables

As discussed in Chapter 2, all variables declared within a subprogram, except for the arguments, are local to that subprogram and have no meaning outside it. For example, suppose that a local variable Z is used in a subroutine as illustrated by

```
SUBROUTINE SUB(X,Y)
    ⋮
   Z = X + Y
    ⋮
END
```

Upon exiting from the subroutine the value of Z may be lost, even to the subroutine itself. Sometimes it is desirable to save certain values between subroutine calls, and this may be accomplished by a SAVE command. (Not all Fortran systems destroy local variables upon termination of a subprogram, in which case the SAVE command would not be necessary.) For example, the construction

```
SUBROUTINE SUB(X,Y)
REAL X, Y, Z
SAVE Z
    ⋮
```

will cause values of Z to be saved between calls of the subroutine, although these values are still local to the subprogram. Thus, if Z=2.5 is computed during the first call of SUB, Z's value will still be 2.5 when the subroutine is called a second time. This feature may be useful for program testing if we wish, for example, to count the number of times a subprogram has been called. We could then add (probably only temporarily) the statements

```
INTEGER N
SAVE N
DATA N/1/
    ⋮
PRINT *, N
N = N + 1
    ⋮
```

and the Nth time the subprogram is called, N would be printed. Note that in this construction N is initialized to 1 by the DATA statement at compilation so that N is not reinitialized each time the subprogram is called.

Passing Information to Subprograms

We now discuss in more detail how information is passed to and from subprograms. Figure 3.6.2 reproduces the first three lines of Figure 3.5.2, the subroutine for matrix-vector multiplication. In this subroutine, N, X, and A are input variables, and B is the output.

Suppose that the MATVEC subroutine is called from the main program by

$$\text{CALL MATVEC(C, U, V, M)} \tag{3.6.5}$$

where we assume for now that the arrays have been declared by

$$\text{REAL C(100,100), U(100), V(100)} \tag{3.6.6}$$

and that the value of M is 100 when (3.6.5) is executed. This value of M is passed to the subroutine and will be used in place of N throughout the subroutine; this is termed *call by value*. For the arrays, however, only their beginning address, plus the first dimension of C, is passed to the subroutine; this is termed *call by reference* or *call by address*. Thus, no additional storage is required by the subroutine for the arrays, nor are any array values passed to the subroutine: the subroutine simply uses the storage defined in the main program for these arrays. This is why arrays may be declared with variable dimensions within a subprogram. In fact, on some systems it makes no difference at all what lengths are given to the arrays X and B

```
SUBROUTINE MATVEC(A,X,B,N)
    INTEGER I, J, N
    REAL A(N,N), X(N), B(N)
```

FIGURE 3.6.2
A subroutine heading

in Figure 3.6.2; X could be declared as X(1), X(100), X(10,000) or even X(*). The only information required by the compiler is that it is a one-dimensional array.

Two-dimensional arrays are different, however, and require caution. In the MATVEC subroutine, the array is used in the statement

$$B(I) = B(I) + A(I,J) * X(J) \tag{3.6.7}$$

The address for A(I,J) is computed within the subroutine by

$$BASE + N * (J-1) + I \tag{3.6.8}$$

where N is the number of rows in the array. (See Section 3.5, and (3.5.11) in particular.) The value N in (3.6.8) corresponds to the declaration A(N,N) in Figure 3.6.2 and is replaced by the current value of M when the subroutine is called by (3.6.5). As long as M is the same as the dimension of the array C declared in the main program, there is no problem, but we next give an example where problems can arise.

Assume that U, V, and C are still declared by (3.6.6). Then, in the main program the statements

```
      DO 1 I = 1, 2
       V(I) = 0
       DO 2 J = 1, 2
        V(I) = V(I) + C(I,J) * U(J)
2      CONTINUE
1      CONTINUE
```

will compute the product of the first 2×2 submatrix of C and the first 2 components of U. But if we tried to accomplish this by

$$CALL\ MATVEC(C,U,V,2) \tag{3.6.9}$$

we would have an error. This is because the subroutine assumes that the array C is 2×2 and uses the first four elements of the actual C, which are the first four elements of the first column of C. Thus, it uses the submatrix

$$\begin{bmatrix} C(1,1) & C(3,1) \\ C(2,1) & C(4,1) \end{bmatrix}$$

rather than the correct submatrix. If we wish the subroutine to be general enough to handle this use of submatrices, we need to have an additional parameter in the calling sequence to specify the dimensions of the array. Thus, we could change the first three statements in Figure 3.6.3 to

```
      SUBROUTINE MATVEC(A,X,B,N,M)
      INTEGER I, J, N, M
      REAL A(M,M), X(M), B(M)
```

```
FUNCTION F(X,Y,Z)
REAL X,  Y,  Z,  F
  F = X + Y * Z
END
```

FIGURE 3.6.3
A simple function

and the call statement (3.6.9) to

```
CALL MATVEC(C,U,V,2,100)
```

Now enough information is passed to the subroutine to allow it to access the correct submatrix of C.

We consider one more aspect of passing array information to subprograms. Suppose that C and V have again been declared by (3.6.6), and that D is also a two-dimensional array declared by

```
REAL D(100,100)
```

Now suppose that we wish to call MATVEC with the vector X to be the Ith column of D. This can be achieved by the call statement

```
CALL MATVEC (C,D(1,I), V,N)
```

The beginning address of the Ith column of D will then be passed to the subroutine, and the effect is that this column becomes the vector X in the subroutine. Note that we cannot do the same thing with a row of D. If D(1,I) were replaced by D(I,1) in the subroutine call, the address of D(I,1) would be passed to the subroutine, but the elements of the Ith row are not the next N elements in storage, since D is stored by column.

Inefficiencies in Subprograms

The discussion on passing information to subprograms applies equally to functions, as well as subroutines. Consider the simple function shown in Figure 3.6.3 and suppose it is invoked by the statement

```
Q = F(R,S,100.0)
```

Then the value of 100.0 for Z, and either the actual values of R and S or their addresses, must be passed to the function. In either case, data must be sent to the subprogram. If addresses are sent, the machine language instructions that implement the arithmetic statement in the function must be modified so that they use R and S. Moreover, transfer operations must be executed to pass control to the subprogram and return to the main program. Thus, use of subprograms entails a certain amount of overhead.

One important advantage of the statement function is that the compiler writes the machine language instructions to evaluate the function directly into the program where it is invoked. This eliminates the overhead in calling a function written as in Figure 3.6.3. However, one important trade-off here is that at each place in the program where the function is used, the instructions will be rewritten. Thus, if the function is used in many different places, more memory will be required than with the function written only once, as in Figure 3.6.3. This is an example of the trade-off between speed and memory, which has always been a consideration in scientific and engineering computation.

Of course, statement functions can only be used in limited circumstances, but it is possible to eliminate the overhead for more complicated functions and subroutines in the following way. As we have discussed, in developing a program it is good practice to break it up into as many modules as feasible; many of these modules will be functions and subroutines. After the program is running correctly, we can then examine places in the program where it would be desirable for efficiency to write a subroutine or function *in-line*. By this we mean that where a particular function or subroutine is called in the main program, the call would be replaced by the code for the subprogram. An example of this is shown in Figure 3.6.4, in which all input/output statements have been omitted. We note that some compilers, especially for rather powerful computers, will automatically perform in-lining of some subprograms, if this leads to greater efficiency.

There are some obvious trade-offs in putting subprograms in-line. First, if the subprogram is at all long and is invoked many times, it is tedious to write it out repeatedly in the main program. Second, the modular

```
PROGRAM EX                      PROGRAM EX
REAL W, X, Y, Z                 REAL W, X, Y, Z
Y = F(X)                        IF (X.LT.0) THEN
Z = F(W)                           Y = X ** 3
END                             ELSE
FUNCTION F(Q)                      Y = Y * Y
   REAL F, Q                    ENDIF
   IF (Q.LT.0) THEN             IF (W.LT.0) THEN
      F = Q ** 3                   Z = W ** 3
   ELSE                         ELSE
      F = Q * Q                    Z = W * W
   END IF                       END IF
END                             END
```

(a) Before   (b) After

FIGURE 3.6.4
Before and after inlining a function

structure of the program tends to be obscured, and the program becomes longer and may be more difficult to understand. However, it is rarely necessary to worry about the loss of efficiency from using subprograms except in critical parts of the program, the so-called "inner loops". (A general rule of thumb that applies to many large programs is that over 90% of the time is consumed by fewer than 10% of the statements.) As an extreme example, suppose that the arithmetic statement (3.6.7) of the MATVEC subroutine (Figure 3.5.2) was implemented by calling the function of Figure 3.6.3. Thus, in place of (3.6.7) in the subroutine there would be the statement

```
B(I) = F(B(I), A(I,J), X(J))
```

and this function will be called for every value of I and J, a total of N^2 times. Clearly, this is the critical part of the multiplication process, and we do not wish to tolerate the inefficiency of a function call at this key point. Moreover, in this particular example, it would be rather absurd to use a function for the simple calculation of (3.6.7), since this would tend to obscure the program.

MAIN POINTS OF SECTION 3.6

- Functions (other than statement functions) may be formal arguments of subprograms. Such functions must be declared as EXTERNAL (or INTRINSIC) in the calling program.

- Values of local variables in subprograms may be lost upon exit. They may be retained by use of the SAVE statement.

- When a subprogram is called, actual variables in the calling sequence are passed by value or reference. In the latter case, only the address is passed, and this is always the case for one-dimensional arrays. For two-dimensional arrays, the beginning address and the number of rows are passed.

- Subprograms have inefficiencies caused by the need to transfer to and from the subprogram, to send data and/or addresses to the subprogram, and to set up proper addresses within the subprogram to access the actual arguments. One advantage of statement functions is that they are compiled in-line and do not suffer these inefficiencies. Other subprograms can also be put in-line if it is important that the overall program be as efficient as possible.

EXERCISES 3.6

3.6.1. Give the value of the output variable Y if the following subroutine is called with X=1.0.

```
SUBROUTINE QU(X,Y,F)        FUNCTION F(X)
REAL X, Y, F                  REAL F, X
EXTERNAL F                    F = 1.0 + X*X
WHILE (F(X).LE.2.0) DO      END
   X = X + 1.0
END WHILE
Y = F(X)
END
```

3.6.2. Complete the program skeleton of Figure 3.6.1 by writing specific functions for R and Q, and additional specific statements for the subroutine. Add to the main program suitable READ and PRINT statements and run the complete program. Then modify the main program so that the subroutine calls replace R and Q by the intrinsic functions SIN and EXP.

3.6.3. Let

$$A = \begin{bmatrix} 1 & 2 & 3 \\ 2 & 3 & 4 \\ 4 & 5 & 6 \end{bmatrix}, \mathbf{x} = \begin{bmatrix} 1 \\ 2 \\ 3 \end{bmatrix}$$

Use these as input to the subroutine of Figure 3.5.2 (see Exercise 3.5.1). Next, with A declared by REAL A(3,3), call the subroutine of Figure 3.5.2 by

CALL MATVEC (A,X,B,2)

with the intent of computing the product

$$\begin{bmatrix} 1 & 2 \\ 2 & 3 \end{bmatrix}\begin{bmatrix} 1 \\ 2 \end{bmatrix}$$

Show that this fails, and then modify the subroutine and call statement, as discussed in the text, so that it works correctly.

3.6.4. For the program and function given below

```
REAL X, Y              REAL FUNCTION F(X)
   Z = F(X)               REAL X
   W = F(Y)               F = X ** 5 + 10.0 * X
END                    END
```

rewrite the program by inlining the function F.

3.6.5. Rewrite the integration program of Figure 2.6.6 so that at each stage the current N is replaced by 2N+1, rather than doubling N. For an initial N=1, show that this corresponds to halving H at each stage. Now note that the integration program is inefficient, since each time the subroutine of Figure 2.6.5 is called it computes all the values of f for the current value of N, even though half of them were computed for the previous value of N. Rewrite the subroutine, using the SAVE statement, so that only new values of f need to be computed.

3.7

CHARACTER COMPUTATIONS

Fortran was designed for numerical computation, but it does contain some features that are useful for "symbol manipulation" or other nonnumerical tasks.

Consider the following problem. Write a program that will accept as input a list of English words and output the number of occurrences of each letter of the alphabet in the list. In order to perform this type of problem it would be highly desirable to be able to perform operations on letters, not just numbers. Fortran allows this by means of another data type, called *character* data. The declaration

$$\text{CHARACTER A, B} \qquad (3.7.1)$$

defines A and B to be *character variables*, and they may be assigned characters as values. For example, the assignment statements

$$\text{A = 'T', \quad B = '='} \qquad (3.7.2)$$

assign the characters T and = to the variables A and B respectively. The allowable characters in Fortran 77 are the digits $0, \ldots, 9$, the letters of the alphabet, A – Z, blanks, commas, and the symbols +, -, *, /, =, ;, ., :, (,), \$.

Strings

In most situations, we would like to work with not only single characters, but *strings* of characters. The following modification of (3.7.1) declares C and D to be strings of 10 characters each:

$$\text{CHARACTER*10, C, D} \qquad (3.7.3)$$

The variables C and D may then each be assigned up to 10 characters, as in

$$\text{C = 'THIS IS IT'} \qquad (3.7.4a)$$
$$\text{D = 'TWENTY'} \qquad (3.7.4b)$$

As illustrated in both (3.7.2) and (3.7.4), a character string in an assignment statement must be enclosed by '. Also, blanks count as characters, as in (3.7.4a), so that this string is a full 10 characters. In (3.7.4b) only six characters are assigned to D; these are left-justified and the right-most four characters in D are *padded* with blanks. On the other hand, if C had only been declared to be six characters, the statement (3.7.4a) would have *truncated* the string to the first six characters: THIS I.

Alternative forms of (3.7.1) and (3.7.3) are

```
CHARACTER *1, A, B                              (3.7.5a)
CHARACTER * 10, C, D, A*1, B*1                  (3.7.5b)
```

In (3.7.5a), the length is specified to be 1; thus, (3.7.5a) is equivalent to (3.7.1). In (3.7.5b), C and D are again of length 10, but the *1 attached to A and B overrides the general specification of 10 characters, and declares A and B to be of 1 character each; thus, (3.7.5b) is equivalent to (3.7.1) and (3.7.3) together.

Reading and Printing Strings

We have previously printed strings of characters in statements such as

```
PRINT *, 'THIS IS IT'                           (3.7.6)
```

Alternatively, we may print string variables using the *A-descriptor*. For example, if C has been assigned the string of (3.7.4a), then the statements

```
    PRINT 10, C                                 (3.7.7a)
10  FORMAT(A10)                                  (3.7.7b)
```

prints the same message as (3.7.6). The A-descriptor has the general form nAw, where w is the number of characters to be printed and n specifies that Aw is repeated n times, just as with the other descriptors. The w may be omitted from the specification, in which case the number of characters printed will be determined by the string length. For example, the 10 may be omitted in (3.7.7b) and 10 characters will still be printed if C has been declared by (3.7.5b). On the other hand, if A10 is replaced by A20 in (3.7.7b), there will be 10 leading blanks before C is printed. And if A10 is replaced by A6, only the 6 leading characters of C will be printed.

Similarly, we may write strings to an output file. For example, the statements

```
        OPEN (7, FILE = 'OUT')
        WRITE (7,100) C, D
100     FORMAT(A10/A10)
```

will write the strings C and D of (3.7.4) to the file OUT, to be printed as

```
THIS IS IT
TWENTY
```

Likewise, we may read strings from the keyboard. If we have the statements

```
CHARACTER * 6, S
READ *, S
```

a string of 6 characters will be expected from the keyboard. Note that this string of characters must be enclosed by '. If we wish to avoid typing these quotation marks, we may use a format, as in

```
READ '(A6)', S
```

or

```
        READ 10, S
10      FORMAT(A6)
```

Then we would not need to enclose the input from the keyboard in quotation marks.

Extraction

In order to do something such as count the number of occurrences of the letter A in a string, we need to be able to extract individual characters or, more generally, substrings. Suppose we have two strings S and T declared by

```
CHARACTER S*6, T*1
```

Thus, S is six characters long and T is one character. Then the operation

$$T = S(3:3) \tag{3.7.8}$$

assigns to T the third character of S and

$$T = S(I:I) \tag{3.7.9}$$

assigns to T the Ith character of S. Thus, for example, if

$$S = 'ABCDEF' \tag{3.7.10}$$

(3.7.8) assigns 'C' to T, and if I = 5 when (3.7.9) is executed, 'E' would be assigned to T.

The operations (3.7.8) and (3.7.9) are special cases of the more general *extraction* of substrings illustrated by

$$T = S(I:J)$$

where we now assume that T is a string of several characters. In this case, the substring of T consisting of characters I through J (counting from the left) would be assigned to T. For example, if S is again given by (3.7.10),

```
T = S(2:4)
```

would assign 'BCD' to T. If we wish the beginning or ending part of a string, we may use the forms

```
S(:J)   or   S(I:)
```

which denote the substrings of characters through the Jth and from the Ith on, respectively.

We next give a simple example in Figure 3.7.1 in which we count the number of occurrences of the letter A in a given string.

The example of Figure 3.7.1 is easily modified to search for particular words, not just letters. For example, if we replace the DO loop in Figure 3.7.1 by that of Figure 3.7.2. we will count the number of appearances of the string DOG. Note that the code in Figure 3.7.2 will also count an occurrence of DOG when it is part of a longer word such as DOGGY. But the code is easily modified to count only occurrences of DOG as a separate word (Exercise 3.7.5).

As a modification of this example, we might wish to know where in the string DOG first appears. We could easily modify the program of Figure 3.7.2 to achieve this (Exercise 3.7.5), but there is a useful intrinsic function, INDEX, that does it directly. If T is a string of no more characters than S, the statement

$$J = INDEX(S, T) \qquad\qquad (3.7.11)$$

will assign to J an integer that is the position of the first occurrence of T in

```
        CHARACTER * 20, S
        READ '(A20)', S
        INTEGER COUNT, I
        COUNT = 0
        DO 10 I = 1, 20
          IF ('A'.EQ.S(I:I)) THEN
            COUNT =  COUNT + 1
          END IF
10      CONTINUE
        PRINT 2, S, COUNT
 2      FORMAT (1X, A20, 4X, I2)
        END
```

FIGURE 3.7.1
Counting occurrences of a letter

```
        DO 10 I = 1, 18
          IF ('DOG'.EQ.S(I:I+2)) THEN
            COUNT = COUNT + 1
          END IF
10      CONTINUE
```

FIGURE 3.7.2
Counting occurrences of a string

S. For example, if

$$T = 'DOG', \qquad S = 'THIS IS A DOG'$$

then statement (3.7.11) will assign the integer 11 to J. If the string T does not appear as a substring in S, the value 0 will be assigned to J.

Concatenation

Suppose we have strings declared by

```
CHARACTER * 5, S, T, U*10
```

so that S and T each have 5 characters and U has 10. Then the statement

```
U = S // T
```

will set U to the *concatenation* of S and T; that is, the first five characters of U will be those of S and the second five those of T. For example, if

$$S = 'ABCDE', \qquad T = 'UVWXY'$$

then

```
U = 'ABCDEUVWXY'
```

As another example, the statement

```
S = T(3:4) // U(5:7)
```

will concatenate the third and fourth characters of T with the fifth, sixth, and seventh characters of U.

Arrays of Strings

Just as with numbers, we may define arrays of strings. For example, the statement

```
CHARACTER *10, U(20), V(20,20), W(-5:5)
```

declares U to be an array with indices $1, \ldots, 20$, W an array with indices $-5, -4, \ldots, 5$, and V to be a two-dimensional array. In this example, all the strings in the arrays have 10 characters each. In general, all the strings of an array must have the same number of characters.

The notation for extracting a substring of an array element is illustrated by

```
U(3)(3:5)
```

which denotes the substring of characters 3, 4, and 5 in the string U(3). Similarly,

```
V(3,4)(4:5) // W(0)(5:5)
```

is the concatenation of characters 4 and 5 in the string V(3,4), with character 5 from the string W(0).

We now give an example that is a typical task of text editors, such as word processors, or the editor that you are using to create your Fortran programs. We assume we have an array S of strings, and we wish to replace the first occurrence of DOG in each string by POOCH. The program to do this is given in Figure 3.7.3. Input and output are not shown in this example.

In Figure 3.7.3, the INDEX function sets J equal to the position of the first occurrence of DOG in S(I). If DOG does not appear in S(I), J is set to 0, nothing more is done, and the DO loop moves to S(I+1). Otherwise, characters J, J+1, and J+2 in S(I) contain DOG, and these are replaced by POOCH by concatenating the first J−1 characters of S(I) with POOCH and the remaining characters of S(I) from position J+3 on. Note that if J=1, S(I)(:0) denotes a null string so that the first five characters of the new S(I) are POOCH. We are tacitly assuming, in this example, that the original strings are no more than 18 characters so that there is room to expand to the full 20 characters (see Exercise 3.7.6).

```
      CHARACTER *20, S(100)
      CHARACTER DOG*3, POOCH*5
      INTEGER I, J
      DOG = 'DOG'
      POOCH = 'POOCH'
      DO 10 I = 1,100
         J = INDEX(S(I), DOG)
         IF (J.NE.0) THEN
            S(I) = S(I)(:J-1)//POOCH// S(I)(J+3:18)
         END IF
10    CONTINUE
```

FIGURE 3.7.3
Replacing a word in a string

Other Intrinsic Character Functions

In addition to the INDEX function, there are some other useful intrinsic functions for characters. The function

        LEN (C)   (3.7.12)

returns an integer that is the length of the character string C, including leading or trailing blanks. If C is declared by, say,

        CHARACTER *6, C   (3.7.13)

then (3.7.12) will return 6. Thus, LEN gives no more information than (3.7.13). However, suppose that throughout the program there are a number of constructions that rely on the length of C, for example,

        DO 10 I = 1, 6   (3.7.14)

where 6 is the string length of (3.7.13). If we wished to change the length in (3.7.13) from 6 to 8 we would need to change all occurrences such as (3.7.14), where the string length has been used. If we write (3.7.14) as

        DO 10 I = 1, LEN(C)

and likewise for all other places the string length appears, then we do not need to worry about changes in the length of C; they will be handled automatically.

A number of other intrinsic functions depend on the *collating sequence* of characters. Assuming that characters are represented in the ASCII convention (see Appendix 1), the collating sequence is just the ordering of the binary representation of the characters. For example, A is represented by 1000001, which is 65 in decimal, and 8 by 0111000, which is 56 in decimal. Thus, $8 < A$ in the collating sequence. The intrinsic function CHAR(I) gives the character in the Ith position of the collating sequence; that is, CHAR(I) gives the character whose binary representation corresponds to the decimal integer I. For example, CHAR(65) is A and CHAR(97) is *a*. (See Appendix 1.) Conversely, the integer function ICHAR(C) gives the numerical representation of the character C; for example, ICHAR(A) is 65 and ICHAR(!) is 33. Thus, all the information in Appendix 1 may be retrieved by using the CHAR and ICHAR functions.

The character C1 is said to be *lexically less than* the character C2 if

        ICHAR(C1) < ICHAR(C2) .

The logical intrinsic function LLT(C1,C2) returns the value TRUE if C1 is lexically less than C2, and FALSE otherwise. For example, LLT(A,8) is

FALSE since the numerical representations of A and 8 are 65 and 56, respectively. The functions LGE, LLE, and LGT give corresponding comparisons for greater than or equal to, less than or equal to, and greater than.

MAIN POINTS OF SECTION 3.7

- Character is another data type. Strings of characters may be declared by constructions such as CHARACTER*10, C, D. Arrays of strings may also be declared.

- Character data may be read and printed using the A format descriptor.

- Characters may be extracted from strings by constructions such as T=S(3:3), and strings may be concatenated by the operator //.

- INDEX, LEN, CHAR, ICHAR, LLE, LGE, LLT, LGT are useful character intrinsic functions.

EXERCISES 3.7

3.7.1. If S, T, and U are character strings declared by

        CHARACTER*5,S,T,U*1

and S='ABCDE', give T after the following statements. Use b for blanks.

(a) T = S(2:3)
(b) U = S(:1)
     T = S(2:)//U

3.7.2. If V is declared by

        CHARACTER*3, V(3)

indicate (by c for character and b for blank) how the output will look from the statements

              PRINT 10, V
        10   FORMAT(2A5)

3.7.3. Write a logical function that will accept as input a string S of 80 characters and a test string of three characters, and output the value .TRUE. if the test string occurs in the string S, and .FALSE. otherwise.

3.7.4. Using the binary (or decimal) representations in Appendix 1, write a logical function that will accept two characters and return the value .TRUE. if the first character is less than the second character, and .FALSE. otherwise.

3.7.5. Modify the programs of Figures 3.7.1 and 3.7.2 so that they find the first occurrence of A and DOG in the string S(I), without using the

INDEX function. Also modify the code of Figure 3.7.2 so that it will count only occurrences of DOG as a separate word, and not as a part of a larger word.

3.7.6. Modify the program of Figure 3.7.3 so that the original strings S(I) may contain up to 20 characters, and if the first occurrence of 'DOG' begins in positions 17 or 18, an error message is produced and the replacement is bypassed.

3.8

MORE ON INPUT/OUTPUT

In Chapter 2, we discussed the I- and F-descriptors for printing integers and floating point numbers. One difficulty with the F-descriptor arises when the magnitudes of the numbers to be printed are much larger or smaller than 1 in absolute value. Consider, for example, the statements

$$
\begin{aligned}
&\texttt{PRINT 100, A} &&\text{(3.8.1a)}\\
&\texttt{100 \quad FORMAT(F20.9)} &&\text{(3.8.1b)}
\end{aligned}
$$

and suppose that on three successive uses of (3.8.1), A has the values

$$6.2, \quad 3.2 \times 10^8, \quad -4.1 \times 10^{-8}. \qquad (3.8.2)$$

Then, the output would be

$$
\begin{aligned}
&\texttt{6.200000000}\\
&\texttt{320000000.000000000} &&\text{(3.8.3)}\\
&\texttt{-0.000000041}
\end{aligned}
$$

Although this output is what you might like for some purposes, it does have drawbacks. Moreover, if the size of the numbers exceeds the particular specification, only an error message would be printed.

The E-Descriptor

An alternative, and usually better, way to print numbers of widely varying magnitudes is in the "scientific notation" of (3.8.2). Fortran represents this notation by printing the numbers of (3.8.2) as

$$\texttt{0.62E+01 \quad 0.32E+09 \quad 0.41E-07} \qquad (3.8.4)$$

In order to print in this form, the F-descriptor in (3.8.1) would be replaced by the *E-descriptor* E9.2.

The basic form of E-descriptor is

```
Ew.d
```

where, just as in the F-descriptor, d is the number of digits to the right of the decimal point and w is the total width of the field. Numbers printed through the E-descriptor always have the normalized form shown in (3.8.4); that is, they begin with 0.x, where x is nonzero. Thus, the width w must be large enough to contain E±xx for the exponent and -0., where the minus appears for negative numbers. Therefore, we must have

$$w \geq d + 7$$

As another example, if the values of the variables U, V, and W are 8124.0, 4.24×10^{-4}, and -2.12×10^{-2}, the statements

```
        PRINT 200, U, V, W
200     FORMAT(1X, E11.4, 2E12.3)
```

will print the line

```
bb0.8124E+04bbb0.424E-03bbb -0.212E-01
```

where b indicates blank. Note that this example shows that an E-descriptor can be repeated, just as an F-descriptor can be repeated, by putting an integer in front of the descriptor.

Output using the E-descriptor is a little ugly, but is probably better than output of the form (3.8.3), and is useful when dealing with numbers of widely varying magnitude. A general rule of thumb is: If you know that all magnitudes of a variable are not dramatically larger or smaller than 1, use the F-descriptor. Otherwise, use the E-descriptor. The general form of the E-descriptor is

```
nEw.d.Ee
```

where e is the number of exponent digits to be printed and n is the number of times the descriptor is repeated. For example, 3E12.4E3 sets up three fields, each having the form

$$\pm 0.xxxxE \pm xxx$$

Note that e=2 corresponds to the standard form. Note also that we now must have $w \geq 5 + e + d$.

Numbers represented in the form (3.8.4) may also be used as constants in arithmetic expressions, for example,

```
X = Y + 0.32E-07
```

In this context, the numbers do not require normalization as in (3.8.4), nor do we need the $+$ sign for a positive exponent, nor the zeros in the exponent. Thus, we might have an expression such as

```
Z = X + 0.02E4 + (Y * 22.4E-7)
```

In general, constants in this exponential form may be used anywhere a constant is appropriate, for example, in PARAMETER or DATA statements.

Double Precision and Complex Numbers

Double precision numbers may be printed using the descriptor Dw.d, where w is the total width of the field and, again, must satisfy $w \geq d + 7$. Normally, the number, d, of digits to the right of the decimal point will be at least eight with the D-descriptor. For example, if X is double precision, the statements

```
        PRINT 100, X
100     FORMAT(1X, D22.14)
```

will print a number such as

```
-  0.12345678987654E+13
```

with 14 digits to the right of the decimal point. As with the E-descriptor, the general form of the D-descriptor is nDw.dEe, where n is the number of times the descriptor is repeated, and e is the number of exponent digits.

Complex numbers may also use the E-descriptor. Thus, if C is complex, the statements

```
        PRINT 100, C
100     FORMAT(1X, 2E14.6)
```

will print the real and imaginary parts of C, each with the descriptor E14.6.

The G-descriptor

The G-descriptor attempts to combine the F- and E-descriptors so as to automatically use the appropriate one. It has the form Gw.d, but the interpretation of this descriptor is different than that of the E- or F-descriptors. Consider the statements

```
        PRINT 10, A
10      FORMAT(1X, G12.3)
```

If A has a magnitude in the range

$$0.1 \leq |A| \leq 10^3 \quad (\leq 10^d, \text{ in general}) \qquad (3.8.5)$$

it will be printed in the F-format, using a field width of w−4, since the exponent will not be printed. Thus, if A = −33.125, it will be printed in this form. But, if (3.8.5) is not satisfied, A will be printed using the E-format. For example, if A = .111 × 10⁻³ or A = 4124.1, these numbers would be printed as

```
0.111E-03      0.412E+04
```

As another example, suppose that

```
A = 1.2345     B= 12.345      C= 123.45
```

Then the statements

```
      PRINT 50, A, B, C
50    FORMAT (1X, 3G10.2)
```

will produce the output

```
1.23     12.34      0.12E+02
```

In the first two cases, A and B are less then 10^2 and the F-descriptor is used, whereas C is greater than 10^2 and uses the E-descriptor.

As indicated by the above discussion, the G-descriptor is a little tricky and its use should be restricted to special situations.

The T-descriptor

The T-descriptor is for "tabs". For example, in the statements

```
      PRINT 50, A, B, C                              (3.8.6a)
50 FORMAT(T31, F6.2, 6X, F6.4, 4X, F6.3)    (3.8.6b)
```

the T31 signifies that all printing is to begin in column 31 and the next descriptor, F6.2, will apply to columns 31 − 36. The effect is the same as if T31 were replaced by 30X.

If the format statement in (3.8.6b) were

```
50    FORMAT(T31, F6.2, T43, F6.4, T53, F6.3)
```

this would signify that the first field begins in column 31, the second field in column 43, and the third field in column 53. This would, in fact, give the same output as (3.8.6b). One advantage of the T-descriptor is that it allows you to specify exactly in what columns the fields should appear without counting spaces and using the X-descriptor.

Reading a File

In Chapter 2, we discussed read statements such as

```
READ *, (A(I), I = 1, 10)
```
(3.8.7)

When (3.8.7) is executed, you will be expected to type in 10 values for $A(1), A(2), \ldots, A(10)$. In many situations, however, you may wish to read a file that has already been prepared in one way or another. If IN is a file holding values for the array A, it may be read by the statements

```
OPEN(9, FILE = 'IN')
READ(9,*) (A(I), I = 1, 10)
```
(3.8.8a)
(3.8.8b)

Just as in our previous use of the OPEN statement in conjunction with the WRITE statement, the statement (3.8.8a) associates 9 in (3.8.8b) with the file IN so that the statement (3.8.8b) now reads this file, rather than receiving input from the keyboard.

Of course, to use the statements (3.8.8) the file IN must contain the appropriate data to be assigned to A. One way this may be accomplished is by a prior WRITE statement, as illustrated in Figure 3.8.1. This is exactly the same construction as used previously to write a file for printer output.

If the program segment of Figure 3.8.1 has been executed, the file IN is saved (perhaps on disk) and may be read later by the statements (3.8.8). In this example, the file IN is written in terms of a format statement, and care must be exercised when using a format statement in this context. Suppose that the format statement in Figure 3.8.1 is changed to

```
10   FORMAT(10F6.1)
```

In this case, the data read into the file IN is rounded (or truncated) to only one decimal digit of accuracy. For example, if A(1) is 2.1245, it would be written to IN as 2.1 and the remaining digits are lost. If this data is to be

```
      REAL A(10)
   Statements to compute A(1), A(2), ..., A(10)
      OPEN(8, FILE = 'IN')
      WRITE(8,10) (A(I), I = 1, 10 )
10    FORMAT(10E15.8)
```

FIGURE 3.8.1
Writing an input file

used for subsequent computation after, say, the READ statement (3.8.8), you probably wish to have it available to full accuracy. This is achieved by the FORMAT statement of Figure 3.8.1, since the specification of 8 digits in the *E*-descriptor retains full accuracy in the data. This would also be achieved by omitting the FORMAT statement in Figure 3.8.1 and changing the WRITE statement to

```
WRITE(8,*)  (A(I),  I = 1,10)
```

This statement then uses the standard format, which gives full accuracy.

End-of-File

In the statement (3.8.8b) it was assumed that we wished to read 10 values into the array A. However, in many situations, we will not know in advance how many values are to be read; we wish to keep reading until the file is exhausted. In this case, the file to be read must have an *end-of-file (EOF)* marker. The program of Figure 3.8.1 would automatically record such an EOF marker after A(10). If there is any doubt that an EOF will be recorded it can be ensured by a statement of the form

```
ENDFILE(UNIT = 8)
```

Assuming that the file to be read has an EOF marker, it can be read with a statement such as

```
READ(9, *, END = 100)  (A(I),  I = 1, 10)
```

in conjunction with the OPEN statement (3.8.8a). This will read values from the IN file until either 10 values have been read or the end-of-file marker is encountered. If the latter, the read statement will be terminated and control transferred to statement 100, which may be the next statement in the program.

In many situations it will be necessary to know how many values have been read before the end-of-file marker is encountered. This can be accomplished by statements such as those shown in Figure 3.8.2. In this example, it is assumed that A is again an array of 10 elements. The WHILE loop will then repeat until either 10 values of A have been read or an end-of-file marker is encountered. In either case, the value of I upon termination of the loop will be the number of values of the array that were read.

Formatted Reads

Just as with PRINT and WRITE statements, the READ statement can also use format statements. However, the interpretation is somewhat

```
I = 0
DO WHILE (I. LT.10)
   READ(9,*, END = 100) A(I+1)
   I = I + 1
END DO
```

FIGURE 3.8.2
Counting elements read

different. Consider the statements

	READ(*,50) X,Y,I	(3.8.9a)
50	FORMAT(F6.2, F12.4, I6)	(3.8.9b)

where it is assumed that X and Y have been declared to be REAL and I is INTEGER. The format statement (3.8.9b) sets up the following fields:

$$|xxxxxx|xxxxxxxxxxxx|xxxxxx|$$

The first field is six wide, the second 12 wide, and the third 6 wide. As opposed to the use of the F-descriptor in output statements, the decimal point does not count for a position in the field width.

Now suppose that the following string of numbers were typed

$$\begin{vmatrix} \text{field 1} \\ 123461 \end{vmatrix} \begin{vmatrix} \text{field 2} \\ bbbb2441241b \end{vmatrix} \begin{vmatrix} \text{field 3} \\ bbb321 \end{vmatrix} \qquad (3.8.10)$$

where b denotes a blank. The first 6 digits correspond to the first field and are read as 1234.61, with the F-descriptor F6.2 defining the position of the decimal point. Similarly, the second number would be read as 244.1241 and the integer as 321. Note that the trailing blank in the second field is ignored. Note also that the decimal point is *not* typed in (3.8.10); its position is implied by the F-descriptor. In fact, if a decimal point is typed, it overrides the F-descriptor. For example, if we typed 12.345 in the first field, this is the value that would be read; however, these fields must be wide enough to accommodate the decimal point if it is typed.

E-descriptors may also be used in the FORMAT statement, in a similar way. However, data in E form may also be used in conjunction with the F-descriptor. For example, if we typed

bbbbb42.1E+9

in the second field of (3.8.10), this would be read as 42.1×10^9. The $F-$descriptor still describes the field width, so that this number would not fit in the first field. However, it is permissible (but not recommended) to eliminate the E if a $\pm$ sign appears before the exponent. Thus, we could type

42.1+9   or   42.1-9

in the first field and, again, this would be read as 42.1×10^9 or 42.1×10^{-9}.

MAIN POINTS OF SECTION 3.8

- The E-format descriptor allows printing of floating point numbers in the form 0.1243E-02. It can be used in place of the F-descriptor when the numbers differ considerably from 1 in absolute value.

- Additional format descriptors are the D-descriptor for double precision numbers, the G-descriptor for combining the E- and F-formats, and the T-descriptor for tabs.

- Input may be obtained by reading files. A READ may be terminated by an end-of-file marker.

- Formats may be used in conjunction with READ statements to set prescribed field widths.

EXERCISES 3.8

3.8.1. Show the output from the following PRINT statement for the values A=-410.1, I=2, J=101. Use b or _ to show blanks.

```
          PRINT 10, 'A(I,J) = ', A, I, J
    10    FORMAT(3X, A7, 2X,E10.3, 3X,2I4)
```

3.8.2. For $A = 412.464$, $B = 3.12 \times 10^6$, and $C = 0.0024 \times 10^{-4}$, give the PRINT and FORMAT statements so that these numbers will be printed in E-format, retaining only the significant digits shown.

3.8.3. For the numbers of Exercise 3.8.2, show the output from the statements

```
          PRINT 10, A, B, C
    10    FORMAT(1X, 3G12.4)
```

3.8.4. Change the format statement in Exercise 3.8.2, using the T-descriptor, so that A will be printed starting in column 20, B in column 35, and C in column 50.

3.8.5. Add a suitable READ or other statements to the program seqment of Figure 3.8.1 to give values to A(1), ..., A(10). Then use the statements of (3.8.8) to read the file IN. Also, read the file IN by the construction shown in Figure 3.8.2.

3.8.6. Using the statements (3.8.9), read the data $X = 32.41$, $Y = 4314.8142$, $I = 232$ without using any decimal points. Read the data again, left-justifying X and Y in their fields and using decimal points. Use suitable PRINT statements to verify that your data has been entered correctly in each case.

3.8.7. Assume that the array declared by REAL A(2,2) holds the values

```
     A(1,1) = 1.23        A(1,2) = 2.14
     A(3,1) = 3.11        A(2,2) = 4.12
```

Give the output for each of the two PRINT sequences:

(a)
```
        DO 1 I = 1,2
            PRINT 10,  (A(I,J),J=1,2)
    10      FORMAT(1X,4E10.2)
    1       CONTINUE
```

(b)
```
            PRINT 10,A
    10  FORMAT(1X,  4E10.1)
```

3.9

SCIENTIFIC COMPUTING: LINEAR EQUATIONS

We now consider one of the most important problems in scientific and engineering computation: the solution of linear systems of equations. The dual goals of this section are to present and discuss the Gaussian elimination method of solving linear systems, and to show how a program that uses this method may be written in a modular fashion. We begin with an example of how a linear system arises.

Least Squares Approximation

In many problems in science and engineering, we wish to approximate a set of data by a "best fit". As a very simple example, suppose that we have m measurements $w_1, \ldots, w_m$ of the weight of some object, perhaps obtained with m different scales. What shall we take as the "best" approximation, w, to the true weight, based on this data? The "principle of least squares approximation" says we should minimize the sum of the squares of the deviations $w - w_i$; that is, we should minimize

$$g(w) = \sum_{i=1}^{m}(w - w_i)^2. \tag{3.9.1}$$

From calculus, we know that g takes on a relative minimum at a point w that satisfies $g'(w) = 0$ and $g''(w) \geq 0$. Since

$$g'(w) = 2\sum_{i=1}^{m}(w - w_i), \quad g''(w) = 2m,$$

it follows that we can find the minimizing value by solving the equation

$$2\sum_{i=1}^{m}(w - w_i) = 0.$$

This gives

$$w = \frac{1}{m}\sum_{i=1}^{m} w_i,$$

so that the best least squares approximation is just the average of the measurements.

The same idea can be applied to obtaining functions that approximate given data. For example, suppose that we measure the temperature of some object as a function of time, and we obtain temperatures $u_1, \ldots, u_m$ at the times $t_1, \ldots, t_m$. Suppose that we know (or assume) that the temperature should obey an equation of the form

$$u(t) = c_1 + c_2 t + c_3 \sin \pi t, \tag{3.9.2}$$

and we wish to estimate the unknown parameters c_1, c_2, and c_3 from the measurements. The least squares principle says that we then should minimize

$$g(c_1, c_2, c_3) = \sum_{i=1}^{m} (c_1 + c_2 t_i + c_3 \sin \pi t_i - u_i)^2 \tag{3.9.3}$$

as a function of c_1, c_2 and c_3.

This problem is a special case of the more general problem: given measurements $u_1, \ldots, u_m$ at times $t_1, \ldots, t_m$, find a function of the form

$$u(t) = c_1 f_1(t) + c_2 f_2(t) + \cdots + c_n f_n(t) \tag{3.9.4}$$

that approximates the data. Here $f_1, \ldots, f_n$ are given functions; for example, for (3.9.2), $f_1(t) = 1, f_2(t) = t, f_3(t) = \sin \pi t$. Again, the parameters $c_1, \ldots, c_n$ in (3.9.4) are to be found by minimizing a sum of squares:

$$\sum_{i=1}^{m} (c_1 f_1(t_i) + c_2 f_2(t_i) + \cdots + c_n f_n(t_i) - u_i)^2. \tag{3.9.5}$$

The quantity to be minimized in (3.9.5) is a function of the n variables $c_1, \ldots, c_n$. Again, we can attack this problem by calculus, but now we must set partial derivatives to zero. We will not give the details of this development, but only state the final result. In order to minimize (3.9.5) and obtain $c_1, \ldots, c_n$, we must solve the system of linear equations

$$\begin{bmatrix} a_{11} & a_{12} & \cdots & a_{1n} \\ a_{21} & & & \vdots \\ \vdots & & & \\ a_{n1} & \cdots & & a_{nn} \end{bmatrix} \begin{bmatrix} c_1 \\ c_2 \\ \vdots \\ c_n \end{bmatrix} = \begin{bmatrix} b_1 \\ b_2 \\ \vdots \\ b_n \end{bmatrix}, \tag{3.9.6}$$

where

$$a_{ij} = \sum_{k=1}^{m} f_i(t_k) f_j(t_k), \quad b_j = \sum_{k=1}^{m} f_j(t_k) u_k. \tag{3.9.7}$$

Gaussian Elimination

In order to solve the linear system of equations (3.9.6), we will use the method of *Gaussian elimination*. We will illustrate this method for the following system of three equations in three unknowns, in which the unknowns are now denoted by x_1, x_2 and x_3. The system

$$\begin{bmatrix} 4 & -9 & 2 \\ 2 & -4 & 4 \\ -1 & 2 & 2 \end{bmatrix} \begin{bmatrix} x_1 \\ x_2 \\ x_3 \end{bmatrix} = \begin{bmatrix} 2 \\ 3 \\ 1 \end{bmatrix} \tag{3.9.8}$$

may be written as

$$\begin{aligned} 4x_1 - 9x_2 + 2x_3 &= 2 \\ 2x_1 - 4x_2 + 4x_3 &= 3 \\ -x_1 + 2x_2 + 2x_3 &= 1 \end{aligned} \tag{3.9.9}$$

The first major step of Gaussian elimination is to eliminate the first variable, x_1, from the second and third equations. If we subtract 0.5 times the first equation from the second equation, and -0.25 times the first equation from the third equation, we obtain the equivalent system of equations:

$$\begin{aligned} 4x_1 - \quad 9x_2 + \quad 2x_3 &= \quad 2 \\ 0.5x_2 + \quad 3x_3 &= \quad 2 \\ -0.25x_2 + 2.5x_3 &= \quad 1.5 \end{aligned} \tag{3.9.10}$$

The second major step eliminates x_2 from the third equation. This is accomplished by subtracting -0.5 times the second equation of (3.9.10) from the third, leading to

$$\begin{aligned} 4x_1 - 9x_2 \quad + 2x_3 &= 2 \\ 0.5x_2 + 3x_3 &= 2 \\ 4x_3 &= 2.5 \end{aligned} \tag{3.9.11}$$

The second part of the algorithm consists of solving the *triangular* system of linear equations (3.9.11). This is easily accomplished by *back substitution*. The last equation of (3.9.11) is

$$4x_3 = 2.5,$$

and, therefore, $x_3 = 2.5/4 = 0.625$. This value now is substituted into the second equation:

$$0.5x_2 + (3)(0.625) = 2;$$

hence, $x_2 = 0.25$. Substitution of x_2 and x_3 into the first equation yields

$$4x_1 - (9)(0.25) + (2)(0.625) = 2,$$

or $x_1 = 0.75$. To check this computed solution, we multiply

$$\begin{bmatrix} 4 & -9 & 2 \\ 2 & -4 & 4 \\ -1 & 2 & 2 \end{bmatrix} \begin{bmatrix} 0.75 \\ 0.25 \\ 0.625 \end{bmatrix}$$

which agrees with the right-hand side of (3.9.8).

For a general $n \times n$ system, Gaussian elimination follows the same steps as for the 3×3 example. If the system is written in the form

$$\begin{aligned}
a_{11}x_1 + \cdots + a_{1n}x_n &= b_1 \\
a_{21}x_1 + \cdots + a_{2n}x_n &= b_2 \\
&\vdots \\
a_{n1}x_1 + \cdots + a_{nn}x_n &= b_n
\end{aligned} \tag{3.9.12}$$

the first stage eliminates the coefficients of x_1 in the last $n - 1$ equations by subtracting a_{21}/a_{11} times the first equation from the second equation, a_{31}/a_{11} times the first equation from the third equation, and so on. This gives the reduced system of equations

$$\begin{aligned}
a_{11}x_1 + a_{12}x_2 + \cdots + a_{1n}x_n &= b_1 \\
a_{22}^{(1)}x_2 + \cdots + a_{2n}^{(1)}x_n &= b_2^{(1)} \\
&\vdots \\
a_{n2}^{(1)}x_2 + \cdots + a_{nn}^{(1)}x_n &= b_n^{(1)},
\end{aligned} \tag{3.9.13}$$

where

$$a_{ij}^{(1)} = a_{ij} - a_{1j}\frac{a_{i1}}{a_{11}}, \quad b_i^{(1)} = b_i - b_1\frac{a_{i1}}{a_{11}}, \quad i, j = 2, \ldots, n.$$

Precisely the same process is now applied to the last $n - 1$ equations of the system (3.9.13) to eliminate the coefficients of x_2 in the last $n - 2$ equations. We continue in this way until the entire system has been reduced to the *triangular system* of equations

$$\begin{aligned}
a_{11}x_1 + a_{12}x_2 + \cdots + \quad a_{1n}x_n &= b_1 \\
a_{22}^{(1)}x_2 + \cdots + \quad a_{2n}^{(1)}x_n &= b_2^{(1)} \\
&\vdots \\
a_{nn}^{(n-1)}x_n &= b_n^{(n-1)}
\end{aligned} \tag{3.9.14}$$

where the superscripts indicate the number of times the elements have, in general, been changed. The solution of the triangular system (3.9.14) is now easily obtained by *back substitution*, in which the equations in (3.9.14) are solved in reverse order:

$$\begin{aligned}
x_n &= \frac{b_n^{(n-1)}}{a_{nn}^{(n-1)}} \\[2mm]
x_{n-1} &= \frac{b_{n-1}^{(n-2)} - a_{n-1,n}^{(n-2)}x_n}{a_{n-1,n-1}^{(n-2)}} \\[2mm]
&\vdots \\[2mm]
x_1 &= \frac{b_1 - a_{12}x_2 - \cdots - a_{1n}x_n}{a_{11}}
\end{aligned} \tag{3.9.15}$$

In the preceding, we have assumed that a_{11} and all of the numbers $a_{ii}^{(i-1)}$, $i = 2, \ldots, n$, that are used as divisors are nonzero.

Input: $n \times n$ matrix A, vector $\mathbf{b}, n$
Reduce system to triangular
    For $k = 1, \ldots, n - 1$,
        If $a_{kk} = 0$, error message and exit
        For $i = k + 1, \ldots, n$
        $\ell_{ik} = \frac{a_{ik}}{a_{kk}}$
          For $j = k + 1, \ldots, n$
            $a_{ij} = a_{ij} - \ell_{ik} a_{kj}$
            $b_i = b_i - \ell_{ik} b_k$
Now solve the triangular system
    If $a_{nn} = 0$, error message and exit
    For $k = n, n - 1, \ldots, 1$
    $x_k = \dfrac{b_k - \sum_{j=k+1}^{n} a_{kj} x_j}{a_{kk}}$

Output: Solution vector $\mathbf{x}$

FIGURE 3.9.1
Pseudocode for Gaussian elimination

The Gaussian elimination process is summarized in the pseudocode of Figure 3.9.1. This pseudocode is written so that as the elements of A are modified, the new elements replace the old ones; likewise for the vector $\mathbf{b}$. Also, the multipliers ℓ_{ik} may be written into the storage locations for a_{ik}, which are no longer needed. If the program is written in this way, the original matrix A and vector $\mathbf{b}$ will be destroyed, which may or may not be what is desired. To keep the original matrix, it must be put into another array before beginning Gaussian elimination.

The pseudocode of Figure 3.9.1 is easily translated into a Fortran program or subroutine for Gaussian elimination (Exercise 3.9.1). Before using such a program, it should be extensively tested; for this, we need systems with known solutions. One easy way to obtain such systems is to choose a matrix A and a solution $\mathbf{x}$, and then form the corresponding $\mathbf{b}$. For example, if

$$A = \begin{bmatrix} 3 & 1 & 1 \\ 1 & 3 & 1 \\ 1 & 1 & 3 \end{bmatrix}, \quad \mathbf{x} = \begin{bmatrix} 1 \\ 2 \\ 3 \end{bmatrix}, \tag{3.9.16}$$

then

$$\mathbf{b} = A\mathbf{x} = \begin{bmatrix} 8 \\ 10 \\ 12 \end{bmatrix}. \tag{3.9.17}$$

Thus, if the vector $\mathbf{b}$ of (3.9.17) and the matrix A of (3.9.16) are given as inputs to the subroutine, the solution vector $\mathbf{x}$ of (3.9.16) should be produced. Also, be sure to test for division by zero. A matrix that will cause this to happen for any vector $\mathbf{b}$ is

$$A = \begin{bmatrix} 1 & 1 & 1 \\ 1 & 1 & 1 \\ 1 & 1 & 1 \end{bmatrix}.$$

Back to Least Squares

We now return to the least squares approximation problem. Given the measurements $u_1, \ldots, u_m$ at the points $t_1, \ldots, t_m$, we first form the matrix A and vector $\mathbf{b}$ of (3.9.6) by the formulas (3.9.7). Then we find the solution of the linear system (3.9.6) by Gaussian elimination; this will produce the coefficients $c_1, \ldots, c_n$ for the approximating function (3.9.4). The overall process is summarized in Figure 3.9.2. A corresponding Fortran program is the subject of Exercise 3.9.2.

The inputs required for the program are the data points $t_1, \ldots, t_m$, the measurements $u_1, \ldots, u_m$ and the functions $f_1, \ldots, f_n$. The latter might be given by function subprograms, perhaps statement functions, or in simple cases such as (3.9.2), they might be written directly in the evaluation of the a_{ij} and b_j. For example, for (3.9.2)

$$f_1(t) = 1, \quad f_2(t) = t, \quad f_3(t) = \sin \pi t \tag{3.9.18}$$

Thus,

$$a_{11} = m, \quad a_{12} = \sum_{k=1}^{m} t_k, \quad a_{13} = \sum_{k=1}^{m} \sin \pi t_k$$
$$a_{22} = \sum_{k=1}^{m} t_k^2, \quad a_{23} = \sum_{k=1}^{m} t_k \sin \pi t_k, \quad a_{33} = \sum_{k=1}^{m} (\sin \pi t_k)^2 \tag{3.9.19}$$

Note that from (3.9.7) $a_{ij} = a_{ji}$ (such a matrix is called *symmetric*) so that the coefficients a_{ij} must only be evaluated for $j \geq i$. In particular, for (3.9.18), the computations of (3.9.19) are sufficient, since $a_{21} = a_{12}, a_{31} = a_{13}$, and $a_{32} = a_{23}$. One way to evaluate the quantities of (3.9.19) is by means of the

Input: $t_1, \ldots, t_m, u_1, \ldots, u_m, f_1, \ldots, f_n$

Step 1. Form the linear system $A\mathbf{c} = \mathbf{b}$:
For $i, j = 1, \ldots, n$
$a_{ij} = \sum_{k=1}^{m} f_i(t_k) f_j(t_k)$
For $i = 1, \ldots, n$
$b_i = \sum_{k=1}^{m} f_i(t_k) u_k$

Step 2. Solve $A\mathbf{c} = \mathbf{b}$ by Gaussian elimination

Output solution: $c_1, \ldots, c_n$

FIGURE 3.9.2
Summary of least squares solution

dot product of Section 2.8 (see Exercises 2.8.3 and 2.8.6). If

$$\mathbf{t} = (t_1, \ldots, t_m), \quad \mathbf{s} = (\sin \pi t_1, \ldots, \sin \pi t_m), \qquad (3.9.20)$$

then a_{22}, a_{23}, and a_{33} are given by the following dot products of the vectors $\mathbf{t}$ and $\mathbf{s}$:

$$a_{22} = (\mathbf{t}, \mathbf{t}), \quad a_{23} = (\mathbf{t}, \mathbf{s}), \quad a_{33} = (\mathbf{s}, \mathbf{s}) \qquad (3.9.21)$$

Although this approach is mathematically pleasing, it would be more efficient to follow the pseudocode of Figure 3.9.3. In this pseudocode, a temporary variable s is used so that only $\sin \pi t_k$ must be evaluated, once for each t_k. It is left to Exercise 3.9.3 to write a Fortran program following the pseudocode of Figure 3.9.3.

We now discuss our overall procedure for the least squares problem. First we broke out a key portion, the solution of a system of linear equations, which we can write as a separate subroutine. In fact, this subroutine can be useful for other problems (although, see the next subsection on errors). In any case, the summary of Figure 3.9.2 does not contain any details of the Gaussian elimination process, which allows us to concentrate on the least squares problem. This is another example of *modular programming*, in which we isolate key portions of the computation into parts that may be handled separately.

Caution must be observed when solving least squares problems. The number of data points, m, must be at least as large as the number of functions, n, or the system of equations (3.9.6) will not have a unique solution. Secondly, even if $n < m$, there still might not be a unique solution, depending on the functions $f_1, \ldots, f_n$; if this is the case, the Gaussian elimination process may encounter a division by zero, which is the reason for the tests for zero in Figure 3.9.1. In this case, a parameter is set showing that Gaussian elimination could not continue and control is passed back to the main program.

Errors in Gaussian Elimination

The Gaussian elimination program of Figure 3.9.1 is suitable for least squares problems because the matrices of such problems are very special.

$$a_{12} = a_{13} = a_{22} = a_{23} = a_{33} = 0$$
For $k = 1$ to m
$$a_{12} = a_{12} + t_k$$
$$a_{22} = a_{22} + t_k^2$$
$$s = \sin \pi t_k$$
$$a_{13} = a_{13} + s$$
$$a_{23} = a_{23} + t_k s$$
$$a_{33} = a_{33} + s^2$$

FIGURE 3.9.3
Pseudocode for evaluation of (3.9.18)

But for general linear systems of equations it can give catastrophic errors. We now examine how this can happen.

Consider the system of linear equations

$$\begin{bmatrix} -10^{-5} & 1 \\ 2 & 1 \end{bmatrix} \begin{bmatrix} x_1 \\ x_2 \end{bmatrix} = \begin{bmatrix} 1 \\ 0 \end{bmatrix}, \tag{3.9.22}$$

whose exact solution is

$$x_1 = -0.4999975 \cdots, \qquad x_2 = 0.999995.$$

Let us carry out Gaussian elimination on (3.9.22) using four digit decimal arithmetic. The multiplier is

$$l_{21} = \frac{0.2 \times 10^1}{-0.1 \times 10^{-4}} = -0.2 \times 10^6,$$

which is exact, and the calculation for the new a_{22} is

$$a_{22}^{(1)} = 0.1 \times 10^1 - (-0.2 \times 10^6)(0.1 \times 10^1) \tag{3.9.23}$$

$$= 0.1 \times 10^1 + 0.2 \times 10^6 \doteq 0.2 \times 10^6.$$

The exact sum in (3.9.23) is 0.200001×10^6, but since we are using only four digits this must be represented as 0.2000×10^6; this is the first error in the calculation. Figure 3.9.4 shows the computed and exact triangular matrices.

The new b_2 is

$$b_2^{(1)} = -(-0.2 \times 10^6)(0.1 \times 10^1) = 0.2 \times 10^6. \tag{3.9.24}$$

No rounding errors occurred in this computation, nor do any occur in the back substitution:

$$x_2 = \frac{b_2^{(1)}}{a_{22}^{(1)}} = \frac{0.2 \times 10^6}{0.2 \times 10^6} = 0.1 \times 10^1,$$

$$x_1 = \frac{0.1 \times 10^1 - 0.1 \times 10^1}{-0.1 \times 10^{-4}} = 0.$$

The computed x_2 agrees with the exact x_2, but the computed x_1 has no digits of accuracy. Note that the only error made in the calculation is in $a_{22}^{(1)}$, which has an error in the sixth decimal place. Every other operation was exact. How, then, can this one "small" error cause the computed x_1 to deviate so drastically from its exact value?

$$\begin{bmatrix} 10^{-5} & 1 \\ 0 & 0.2 \times 10^6 \end{bmatrix} \qquad \begin{bmatrix} 10^{-5} & 1 \\ 0 & 0.200001 \times 10^6 \end{bmatrix}$$

(a) Computed   (b) Exact

FIGURE 3.9.4
Computed and exact triangular matrices

Note that the quantity 0.000001×10^6 that was dropped from the computed $a_{22}^{(1)}$ in (3.9.23) is the original element a_{22}. Since this is the only place that a_{22} enters the calculation, the computed solution would have been the same if a_{22} were zero. Therefore, the calculation using four digits has computed the exact solution of the system

$$\begin{bmatrix} -10^{-5} & 1 \\ 2 & 0 \end{bmatrix} \begin{bmatrix} x_1 \\ x_2 \end{bmatrix} = \begin{bmatrix} 1 \\ 0 \end{bmatrix}. \tag{3.9.25}$$

Intuitively, we would expect the two systems (3.9.22) and (3.9.25) to have rather different solutions, and this is indeed the case. But why did this occur? The culprit is the large multiplier l_{21}, which made it impossible for a_{22} to be included in the sum in (3.9.23), using only four digits. This large multiplier was due to the smallness of a_{11} relative to a_{21}.

We can easily circumvent this problem by simply interchanging the order of the equations:

$$\begin{bmatrix} 2 & 1 \\ -10^{-5} & 1 \end{bmatrix} \begin{bmatrix} x_1 \\ x_2 \end{bmatrix} = \begin{bmatrix} 0 \\ 1 \end{bmatrix}. \tag{3.9.26}$$

If we do Gaussian elimination on (3.9.26) using four digits, we obtain

$$l_{21} = \frac{-0.1 \times 10^{-4}}{0.2 \times 10^1} = -0.5 \times 10^{-5}$$

$$a_{22}^{(1)} = 0.1 \times 10^1 - (-0.5 \times 10^{-5})(1) \doteq 0.1 \times 10^1$$

$$b_2^{(1)} = 0.1 \times 10^1 - (-0.5 \times 10^{-5})(0) = 0.1 \times 10^1$$

$$x_2 = \frac{0.1 \times 10^1}{0.1 \times 10^1} = 1.0$$

$$x_1 = \frac{-(0.1 \times 10^1)(1)}{0.2 \times 10^1} = -0.5.$$

The computed solution now agrees excellently with the exact solution.

This example illustrates that the Gaussian elimination algorithm may give inaccurate results if the multipliers are large. The example also indicates that this difficulty might be remedied by interchanging equations; this is, in fact, the case. By a relatively simple strategy we can always arrange to keep the multipliers in the elimination process less than or equal to 1 in absolute value. This is known as *partial pivoting*: at the kth stage of the elimination process an interchange of rows is made, if necessary, to place in the main diagonal position the element of largest absolute value from the kth column on or below the main diagonal. Figure 3.9.5 gives this modification to the part of the pseudocode of Figure 3.9.1 that reduces the original system to triangular. The back substitution remains the same.

Gaussian elimination with partial pivoting has proved to be an extremely reliable algorithm in practice. However, the matrix must be properly scaled before the algorithm is used. To illustrate this, consider the system

$$\begin{bmatrix} 10 & -10^6 \\ 2 & 1 \end{bmatrix} \begin{bmatrix} x_1 \\ x_2 \end{bmatrix} = \begin{bmatrix} -10^6 \\ 0 \end{bmatrix}, \tag{3.9.27}$$

For $k = 1, \ldots, n - 1$

Find $m \geq k$ such that $|a_{mk}| = \max\{|a_{ik}| : i \geq k\}$.

If $a_{mk} = 0$, then error message and exit.

Else interchange a_{kj} and a_{mj}, $j = k, k + 1, \ldots, n$.

interchange b_k and b_m.

For $i = k + 1, k + 2, \ldots, n$

$l_{ik} = a_{ik}/a_{kk}$

For $j = k + 1, k + 2, \ldots, n$

$a_{ij} = a_{ij} - l_{ik}a_{kj}$

$b_i = b_i - l_{ik}b_k$.

FIGURE 3.9.5
Reduction to triangular system with partial pivoting

which is the original system (3.9.22) with the first equation multiplied by -10^6. (Multiplication of an equation by a constant does not change the solution.) No interchange is called for by the partial-pivoting strategy since the $(1, 1)$ element is already the largest in the first column. However, if we carry out the elimination using four digits (see Exercise 3.9.5), we will encounter exactly the same problem that we did with the system (3.9.22). To avoid this problem, rows of the matrix should be scaled so that the maximum absolute value of the elements in each row is approximately 1. If we do this with (3.9.27), the $(1, 1)$ element will then become small, and the partial-pivoting strategy will cause an interchange of the equations.

Ill-Conditioned Linear Systems

We next give another example that, at first glance, looks like simple rounding error, but there is a deeper root cause. Consider the system

$$0.832x_1 + 0.448x_2 = 1.00$$
$$0.784x_1 + 0.421x_2 = 0, \tag{3.9.28}$$

and assume that we now use three-digit decimal arithmetic to carry out Gaussian elimination. Since a_{11} is the largest element of the matrix, no interchange is required, and the computation of the new elements $a_{22}^{(1)}$ and $b_1^{(1)}$ is

$$l_{21} = \frac{0.784}{0.832} = 0.942\underline{308} \cdots \doteq 0.942$$

$$a_{22}^{(1)} = 0.421 - 0.942 \times 0.448 = 0.421 - 0.422\underline{016} \doteq -0.001 \tag{3.9.29}$$

$$b_2^{(1)} = 0 - 1.00 \times 0.942 = -0.942,$$

where the underscored digits are lost in the computation. Hence, the computed triangular system is

$$0.832x_1 + 0.448x_2 = 1.00$$
$$-0.001x_2 = -0.942,$$

(3.9.30)

and the back substitution produces the approximate solution

$$x_1 = -506, \qquad x_2 = 942.$$

(3.9.31)

But the exact solution of (3.9.28), correct to three figures, is

$$x_1 = -439, \qquad x_2 = 817,$$

(3.9.32)

so the computed solution is incorrect by about 15%. Why has this occurred?

The first easy answer is that we have lost significance in the calculation of $a_{22}^{(1)}$. Indeed, it is clear that the computed value of $a_{22}^{(1)}$ has only one significant figure, so our final computed solution will have no more than one significant figure. But this is only one manifestation of the real problem. By carrying out a more detailed computation we can show that the computed solution (3.9.31) is the exact solution of the system

$$0.832x_1 + 0.447974 \cdots x_2 = 1.00$$
$$0.783744 \cdots x_1 + 0.420992 \cdots x_2 = 0,$$

(3.9.33)

where $\cdots$ in the coefficients indicates that only six figures are shown. The maximum percentage change between the elements of this system and the original system (3.9.28) is only 0.03%; therefore, errors in the data are magnified by a factor of about 500.

Whenever a problem is such that small changes in the data of the problem can cause large changes in the solution, the problem is called *ill-conditioned*. In the case of (3.9.28), small changes (0.03%) in the coefficients of the matrix cause large changes (15%) in the solution. Thus, just because the coefficients in the matrix are accurate to three decimal places, we cannot expect a solution with similar accuracy. The fault is *not* that of the Gaussian elimination algorithm, but of the problem itself.

We can understand geometrically the cause of this ill-conditioning in (3.9.28). Figure 3.9.6 shows a plot of the two equations of (3.9.28). The intersection (not shown) of these two lines is the solution of the system. As shown in Figure 3.9.6 the lines are almost parallel. It is this that causes the ill-conditioning, since very small changes in the slopes of the lines can cause very large changes in their intersection point. In fact, consider the system of equations

$$0.832x_1 + 0.448x_2 = 1.00$$
$$0.784x_1 + (0.421 + \varepsilon)x_2 = 0.$$

(3.9.34)

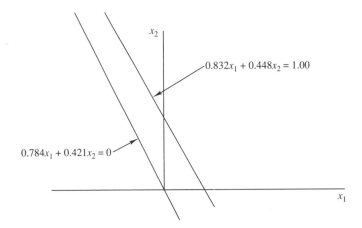

FIGURE 3.9.6
Almost-parallel lines defined by (3.7.28).

The second equation defines a family of lines depending on the parameter ε. As ε increases from zero to approximately 0.0012, the line rotates counterclockwise causing its intersection with the line defined by the first equation to recede to infinity until the two lines become exactly parallel, and no solution of the linear system exists.

Ill-conditioned problems pervade all areas of scientific and engineering computations, not just linear equations. It is necessary to be alert to such possibilities when it appears that an algorithm might be giving errors.

Efficiency

We have previously discussed some inefficiencies in using certain Fortran constructs, such as two-dimensional arrays and subprograms. But these inefficiencies are minor compared to inefficiencies that can result from the use of poor algorithms. We next give an example of how a very inefficient method could arise in the context of linear equations.

Many elementary textbooks on linear algebra present *Cramer's rule* as a method for solving linear systems of equations. This method involves computing quotients of certain determinants of matrices. For 2×2 and 3×3 matrices A, the determinant is given by the formulas

$$n = 2 : \det A = a_{11}a_{22} - a_{12}a_{21}$$
$$n = 3 : \det A = a_{11}a_{22}a_{33} + a_{12}a_{23}a_{31} + a_{13}a_{21}a_{32}$$
$$- a_{11}a_{23}a_{32} - a_{13}a_{22}a_{31} - a_{12}a_{21}a_{33}.$$

For general n, these simple formulas generalize to the sum of all possible products (half with minus signs) of elements of the matrix, with one element from each row and each column. There are $n!$ such products for an $n \times n$ matrix. (In particular, 2 for $n = 2$ and 6 for $n = 3$, as shown above.)

Now, if we carry out the computation of a determinant based on a straightforward implementation of this formula, the process would require about $n!$ multiplications and additions. For n very small, say $n = 2$ or $n = 3$, this is a small amount of work. Suppose, however, that we have a 20×20 matrix, a very small size in current scientific computing. If we assume that each arithmetic operation requires 1 microsecond (10^{-6} second), about the speed of PCs, then the time required for this calculation — even ignoring all overhead operations in the computer program — will exceed 1 million years! On the other hand, the Gaussian elimination method will perform the arithmetic operations for the solution of a 20×20 linear system in less than 0.005 second, again assuming 1 microsecond per operation. Although this is an extreme example, it does illustrate the difficulties that can occur by naively following a mathematical prescription in order to solve a problem on a computer.

In general, we would like to choose a method that minimizes the computing time, yet retains suitable accuracy. For some relatively simple problems, an estimate of the computing time may be based on counting the number of arithmetic operations required. For example, for Gaussian elimination, approximately $\frac{1}{3}n^3$ multiplications and $\frac{1}{3}n^3$ additions are required for large n. (Note the tremendous difference in how rapidly $n!$ grows as compared to n^3: for $n = 20$, $n^3 \doteq 10^4$ but $n! \doteq 10^{18}$.) Is this the best that can be done? For many years it was thought that Gaussian elimination was probably the optimal algorithm, but in 1969 a method was given in which the number of multiplications was proportional to $n^{2.81}$, which is considerably smaller than n^3 for large n. However, this method is much more complicated than Gaussian elimination; only for very large n (for example, $n = 1000$) is it actually faster.

The study of the efficiency of algorithms has led to the subarea of computer science called *computational complexity*. However, only for relatively simple problems is it possible to ascertain precisely how fast a given algorithm will be. Usually, timing comparisons of competitive algorithms must be made in order to determine the most efficient one.

MAIN POINTS OF SECTION 3.9

- Least squares approximation leads to a linear system of equations that can be solved by Gaussian elimination without row interchanges.

- Gaussian elimination may be incorporated into a subroutine and used as part of a larger program. This is an example of modular programming.

- In general, Gaussian elimination can be a very inaccurate algorithm, unless partial pivoting and scaling are incorporated.

- Even with a good algorithm, solution of linear systems may be inaccurate if the system is ill-conditioned.

EXERCISES 3.9

3.9.1. Translate the pseudocode of Figure 3.9.1 into a Fortran subroutine that accepts A, $\mathbf{b}$, and n as inputs, and outputs either the solution vector $\mathbf{x}$ or a logical variable indicating that a divisor was zero.

3.9.2. Write a Fortran program to carry out the least squares algorithm summarized in Figure 3.9.2. Use the Gaussian elimination subroutine of Exercise 3.9.1 and assume that the functions $f_1, \ldots, f_n$ will be given by function subprograms.

3.9.3. Specialize the Fortran program of Exercise 3.9.2 to obtain the least squares approximation for (3.9.2). Use the algorithm of Figure 3.9.3 for the evaluation of the coefficient matrix A. Use the Gaussian elimination subroutine of Exercise 3.9.1 to solve the linear system. Run your program for the data

$$t_1 = 0, t_2 = \frac{1}{4}, t_3 = \frac{1}{2}, t_4 = \frac{3}{4};$$

$$u_1 = 1.5, u_2 = 4.0, u_3 = 5.5, u_4 = 5.0.$$

If you have access to a graphics system, plot the input data and your approximating least squares function.

3.9.4. Modify the Gaussian elimination subroutine of Exercise 3.9.1 so as to incorporate partial pivoting, as given in the pseudocode of Figure 3.9.4.

3.9.5. Using four-digit decimal arithmetic, as done with the example (3.9.22), show that Gaussian elimination fails for the system (3.9.27) in the same way it does for (3.9.22).

4

THE NEW
AND THE OLD

In previous chapters, we have briefly mentioned some Fortran 90 constructs. In Section 4.1, we will review these, as well as additional more or less natural extensions to Fortran 77, and then discuss more advanced features in Section 4.2. We note first that all of Fortran 77 is part of Fortran 90. However, many Fortran 90 changes will make certain Fortran 77 features obsolete. This will be discussed in Section 4.3.

4.1

FORTRAN 90: BASIC CHANGES

The form of a Fortran 90 program is much more general than Fortran 77. There is no longer any restriction (columns 7 – 72) on where statements may appear; the code is completely free-form, and the following are allowed:

- Lines are up to 132 characters long.

- A line may contain multiple statements, separated by semicolons.

- Statements may be continued by adding an ampersand.

- Comments may be placed in-line, preceded by an exclamation mark.

We illustrate some of the above with the following lines of code

```
X = Y + Z;  W = U + V      ! two statements
X =     &
    Y + Z                  ! a continued statement
```

Each program unit (main program or subprogram) must use either the old fixed form or the new free form; they cannot be mixed.

Variables and Declarations

Identifiers are allowed to be up to 31 alphanumeric characters long and may include the underbar _. For example, the following are possible identifiers

```
X_bar,    THIRTYSOMETHING,    A12_12
```

As in Fortran 77, the first character of an identifier must be a letter. But unlike Fortran 77, spaces are significant; for example, PR INT is not PRINT. As in Fortran 77, no differentiation is made between uppercase and lowercase: *Aa* and *aa* are the same identifier.

Variables may be declared with or without double colons, as in

```
REAL R, S    or    REAL :: R, S
```
(4.1.1)

Initialization may be combined with declarations, as in

```
REAL :: R = 7.0, S = 10.1
```
(4.1.2)

and in this case :: must be used. Note that some usefulness of the DATA statement is obviated by this capability. The PARAMETER statement may be written in a similar way, combining the type declaration in the same statement:

```
REAL, PARAMETER :: E = 2.71, PI = 3.14
```

Character data may be declared by

```
CHARACTER(LEN = 20) :: S,T
```

which is equivalent to CHARACTER*20,S,T in Fortran 77. The statement

```
IMPLICIT NONE
```

requires that all variables must be declared. This should always be done, with this statement at the beginning of the program unit.

Arrays may be declared and initialized in a way similar to (4.1.2), although DIMENSION is now used. For example,

```
REAL, DIMENSION(5,5) :: A,B, C(10)
```

declares A and B to be 5×5 two-dimensional arrays and C a 10-long one-dimensional array; note that the specific declaration for C overrides the general declaration that applies to A and B. Initialization may be added to the declaration as illustrated by

```
INTEGER, DIMENSION(3) :: IN = (/1,2,3/)
```

Here, IN is declared to be a 3-long, one-dimensional array with initial values 1, 2, 3. Alternatively, array values may be given in an assignment statement, such as

$$IN = (/1,2,3/) \tag{4.1.3a}$$

or in implied DO loop form

$$IN = (/(I, I = 1, 3)/) \tag{4.1.3b}$$

or in terms of other variables

$$IN = (/ N, M, P(2) /) \tag{4.1.3c}$$

In (4.1.3c), N and M are integer variables and P is an integer array. The sets of values in (4.1.3) are called *array constructors*, and may only be used in this way in one-dimensional arrays. Arrays up to seven dimensions are permitted, as in Fortran 77. Storage by the column-major convention is expected, but not required.

Dynamic Storage Allocation

A major limitation of Fortran 77 is that the actual sizes of all arrays must be declared in the main program. This is called *static storage allocation*: Once declared, sizes of arrays cannot be changed. Fortran 90 allows *dynamic storage allocation* by means of the ALLOCATE statement. For example, the statement

```
REAL, DIMENSION(:,:), ALLOCATABLE :: A
```

declares A to be a two-dimensional array, but does not assign any storage at this point. Later in the program the statement

```
ALLOCATE(A(50,100))
```

allocates storage for a 50×100 array. Integer variables and expressions may also be used in the ALLOCATE statement; for example

```
ALLOCATE(A(N,2*N))
```

allocates storage based on the current value of N. Any integer expression may be used in the subscript positions.

If, at some later point in the program, the array A is no longer needed, its storage may be released by

```
DEALLOCATE(A)
```

At this point, A is still defined as a two-dimensional array, but has no storage assigned; storage may be assigned in the future by another ALLOCATE statement. Storage for several arrays may be allocated in the same statement, for example

```
ALLOCATE(A(10,10), X(N**4), B(20))
```

Similarly, several arrays may be deallocated by the same statement:

```
DEALLOCATE(A,X,B)
```

With dynamic storage allocation, we can be sure that the right amount of space is allocated to arrays without knowing in advance how much is needed. And when storage is no longer needed for some array, deallocation allows that space to be used for other purposes.

Do Loops

The DO loop may be written in the form

```
DO I = 1, N
    Statements
END DO
```
                                                                    (4.1.4)

Note that no CONTINUE statement nor statement number is needed; all statements between DO and END DO are repeated N times. The value of DO loop indices are available upon termination of the loop. For example, in (4.1.4), I will have the value N+1 upon termination.

In nested DO loops it is possible to name the loops so as to make the structure more clear; for example,

```
OUTER: DO I=1,N
    Statements
  INNER: DO J = 1,M
    Statements
  END DO INNER
END DO OUTER
```

If a DO loop is named, the corresponding END DO statement *must* contain the same name.

Array Arithmetic

Much of the usefulness of DO loops concerns operations on arrays and some of this is obviated by *array operations* in Fortran 90. For example, if A and B are two conformable arrays (they are the same shape), then the statement

```
C = A + B
```

computes all the sums of corresponding elements of the arrays, and no DO loop is required. Other examples are

```
C = A + 1.0
```

which adds 1.0 to all elements of A, and

```
C = A * B
```

which assigns to C the products of corresponding elements of A and B.

Array operations are handled by position in the array, not by subscript. For example, if A, B, and C have been declared by

$$\text{REAL A(1:5), B(2:6), C(3:7)} \tag{4.1.5}$$

the statement

```
C = A + B
```

assigns A(I) + B(I+1) to C(I+2), for I = 1,..., 5. The arrays of (4.1.5) are conformable since they are all one-dimensional and have the same length.

In the above examples, the whole arrays are used. But subsets of arrays may also be used in array operations; for example, the statement

```
A(2:4) = 1.0
```

assigns 1.0 to A(2), A(3), and A(4). As another example,

```
A(2:N) = A(1:N - 1)
```

shifts the elements of the array A by one. A step may also be used in such constructions; for example, if A is a 6-long array, the statement

```
A(2:6:2) = 1.0
```

assigns 1.0 to elements A(2), A(4), and A(6). More generally,

```
A(N:M:L) = 1.0
```

has the same effect as the DO loop

```
DO I = N, M, L
   A(I) = 1.0
END DO
```

and the stride L may be either positive or negative. Subsets of arays are called *array sections*.

Similar constructions may be used with two- or higher-dimensional arrays. Also, a vector of subscripts may be used to select elements. For example, suppose that A is a 10×10 array, and U is a 3-long integer array with elements 3, 6, 8. Then

```
A(2:10:2,U)
```

is the subset of all elements of A with first subscript 2, 4, 6, 8, 10, and second subscript 3, 6, 8. We can write this in the alternative way

```
A(2:10:2,(/3,6,8/))
```

in which the vector subscript is explicit. Other useful constructions are given by the following examples. If Y and Z are one-dimensional arrays, the statements

```
Y = A(I, :) ; Z=A(:,J)
```

set Y equal to the Ith row of A, and Z equal to the Jth column of A. The statement

```
Y = A(I, 1:N:3)
```

puts every third element of the Ith row of A into the array Y, and

```
Z = A(I, N:1:-1)
```

sets Z equal to the Ith row of A in reverse. In array operations, the order in which the individual operations are carried out is not specified in the standard, leaving open the best implementation strategies for different computers.

Decision Statements

The IF construct remains the same as in Fortran 77, but in addition to the comparison operators .LT., .LE., and so on, of Fortran 77, the more mathematical representations

```
==,   /=,   <=,   >=,  <,   >
```

are now allowed. Here, the first two symbols represent $=$ and $\neq$, and the third and fourth symbols represent $\leq$ and $\geq$, respectively. An example is

```
IF((I <= J)  .AND.  (K /= M))  Y = A
```

which sets Y =A if $I \leq J$ and $K \neq M$. Another example is

```
TEST: IF (I == N)  THEN
         Y = A
END IF TEST
```

illustrating that, as with a DO statement, an IF statement may be named. (If the IF statement is named, the END IF statement *must* have the same name.)

WHILE, EXIT and CYCLE

The WHILE DO construction was not in the Fortran 77 standard, nor is it in Fortran 90. DO WHILE is, however, part of Fortran 90; for example,

```
DO WHILE (X <= 10.0)
     Statements
END DO
```

is legal. An alternative to the DO WHILE construction is discussed next.

It is possible to have a DO loop with no index or test at all, for example

```
DO
     Statements
IF (X > 10) EXIT
END DO
```

If the argument of the IF statement is true, the DO loop will be terminated and control passed to the statement following END DO. The IF statement need not be the statement before END DO, and may be placed anywhere between DO and END DO. However, clarity is enhanced if EXIT is in either the first or last statement within the DO body. More generally, EXIT NAME exits from the DO block labeled NAME.

A related construction involves CYCLE. For example, in the segment

```
DO I = 1,N
     Statements
IF (X > 10) CYCLE
     Statements
END DO
```

if X > 10, CYCLE bypasses the second group of statements, and the loop then continues by executing the first group of statements with the next higher value of I.

The WHERE Statement

The WHERE statement eliminates the need for an IF statement in certain situations. For example, if A and B are conformable arrays, the statement

```
WHERE (A >= 0) B = SQRT(A)
```

assigns the square roots of the nonnegative elements of A to the corresponding positions of B. This construction also illustrates the use of intrinsic functions applied to arrays. Any intrinsic function may be used in this fashion, as long as it makes sense. For example, if Y and A are conformable arrays

```
Y = SIN(A)
```

will assign the sines of the elements of A to the corresponding positions of Y.

As another example, we may write the compound construction

```
WHERE (A <= 0)
   B = A
ELSEWHERE
   B = 0
END WHERE
```

Here, an element of B is set either to 0 or the corresponding element of A, depending on the sign of that element of A.

The CASE Statement

The selection of one of several possible courses of action may be implemented in Fortran 77 by a nested IF sequence or the ELSE IF construct. In Fortran 90, another way to achieve this is by the CASE statement, new to Fortran, but already in other languages such as C and TRUE BASIC. Consider the following example:

```
SELECT CASE(N)
CASE(1)
      Statements
CASE(2)
      Statements
CASE(6)
      Statements
END SELECT
```

This is equivalent to

```
IF(N==1) THEN
      Statements
ELSE IF(N==2) THEN
      Statements
ELSE IF(N==6) THEN
      Statements
END IF
```

Thus, if the integer variable N is 1, 2, or 6, the statements in the corresponding CASE block are executed and the others bypassed, whereas if N is not one of these integers, all cases are bypassed. Therefore, at most one CASE block is executed.

Ranges of values or lists of values may also be selected, as in

```
SELECT CASE(I)
CASE(-10:-1)
      Statements
CASE(1:10,12,14)
      Statements
CASE DEFAULT
      Statements
END SELECT
```

Here, if $-10 \leq I \leq -1$, the first case is executed, whereas the second case is executed if $1 \leq I \leq 10$, or $I = 12, 14$. The DEFAULT case is executed if neither of the other cases is executed.

Subprograms

As in Fortran 77, subprograms are either functions or subroutines but the word *procedure* is used as a synonym for subprogram. Subprograms are classified as *internal* or *external*. External subprograms are the same as self-contained subprograms in Fortran 77: They are defined outside the main program, and information is passed to and from the subprogram through the calling sequence. Internal subprograms are defined within the main program, or within an external subprogram, and have access to all variables within that program unit. Thus, they are a mechanism for sharing data. Recall that the scope of a variable is the set of statements in which it is defined. Therefore, the scope of a variable defined in a main program is the whole program, plus any internal subprograms.

Internal subprograms may not contain additional subprograms and they must be preceded by a CONTAINS statement. This is illustrated by the program in Figure 4.1.1. The CONTAINS statement, followed by its procedures, appears last in a program. A call to an internal subprogram may only be from within the program unit in which the subprogram is defined. Note that because F is defined as an internal subprogram it has access to the variable W in the main program, even though W is not included in the calling sequence. The END statement of the function must contain the function name whereas the name of the main program in its END statement is optional.

A useful feature for subprograms, partly for readability and partly for preventing and detecting errors, is that dummy variables may be declared as input or output variables, or both. For example, in the declarations

```
SUBROUTINE SUB(W,X,Y,Z)
  REAL, INTENT (IN) :: X,Y
  REAL, INTENT (OUT) :: W
  REAL, INTENT (INOUT) :: Z
```

```
PROGRAM EXAM
  IMPLICIT NONE
  REAL X, Y, Z, W, F
  READ*, X, Y, W
  Z = F(X,Y)
CONTAINS
  FUNCTION F(X,Y)
  REAL X,Y
    F = X *X + Y *Y + W
  END FUNCTION F
END EXAM
```

FIGURE 4.1.1
An internal subprogram

X and Y are declared to be input variables, W an output variable, and Z both input and output. The OUT and INOUT variables *must* be variables (not constants) upon invoking the subprogram, since they are assigned values by the subprogram. The use of the INTENT construct is strongly recommended in all subprograms.

Array sections may be passed to a subprogram, as illustrated by the statement

$$\text{CALL MAT}(A(:,I), B(J,:)) \tag{4.1.6}$$

Here it is assumed that MAT is a subroutine with two one-dimensional arrays as dummy arguments, and A and B are two-dimensional arrays. The statement (4.1.6) passes two array sections, the Ith column of A and the Jth row of B, to the subroutine. As discussed in Section 3.6, a column of a two-dimensional array may be easily passed to a subroutine in Fortran 77, but there is no natural way to pass a row since storage is by columns. This difficulty is overcome in Fortran 90.

Functions

Fortran 90 has several new and useful intrinsic functions. For example,

```
CEILING(X)
```

returns the smallest integer $\geq$ X and

```
FLOOR(X)
```

returns the largest integer $\leq$ X. Additional Fortran 90 intrinsic functions are given in Appendix 2.

A very important change in Fortran 90 is that although a function must still return a single result, this result may now be a whole array. For example, the following function computes the matrix-vector product B = AX. (There is an intrinsic function, MATMUL, for this operation so that the following function is given for the purpose of illustration only.)

```
FUNCTION MM(A,X,N) RESULT(B)
  IMPLICIT NONE
  INTEGER I, J, N
  REAL A(N,N), X(N), B(N)
  DO I = 1,N
    B(I) = 0
    DO J = 1,N
      B(I) = B(I) + A(I,J) * X(J)
    END DO
  END DO
END FUNCTION MM
```

Note that in the function heading a result variable B is defined, and this variable is declared to be an array within the function. (This result variable has nothing to do with B being an array and should be used even when the output is a single scalar.) The array B is internal to the function and the function will be invoked by a statement such as

```
Y = C + MM(A,X,N)
```

where Y and C are N-long one-dimensional arrays. External functions with arrays as output must be used in conjunction with the INTERFACE statement, which will be discussed in Section 4.2.

Recursive functions (functions that call themselves) are illegal in Fortran 77, but are allowed in Fortran 90. For example, the factorial function N! may be defined by:

```
RECURSIVE FUNCTION F(N) RESULT(FAC)
  IMPLICIT NONE
  INTEGER, INTENT(IN) :: N
  INTEGER FAC
  IF (N == 1) THEN
  FAC = 1
  ELSE
  FAC = N * F(N - 1)
  END IF
END FUNCTION F
```

Here, the word RECURSIVE in the function heading is necessary when defining a recursive function. Again, an internal result variable FAC is used, but the function is invoked by the function name F within the function, as illustrated by the statement FAC = N*F(N-1). Even though recursive functions are sometimes elegant, they may also be inefficient.

Formats

Formats may be specified in Fortran 90 by character variables, rather than FORMAT statements. For example, the statement

```
CHARACTER(LEN=8), PARAMETER :: FOR = '(2F10.3)'
```

declares FOR to be a character parameter with value (2F10.3). FOR may then be used to specify the format in WRITE or PRINT statements, as in

```
WRITE(10, FOR) A,B
```

or

```
PRINT FOR, A, B
```

The character variable FOR could also be set by an assignment statement, but declaring it as a parameter is good practice.

MAIN POINTS OF SECTION 4.1

- Fortran 90 programs may be written in "free-form".

- Identifiers may be 31 characters, including an underbar. Initialization of variables may be combined with declarations.

- IMPLICIT NONE should always be used to enforce declarations of all variables.

- Storage for arrays may be allocated and deallocated dynamically. Array arithmetic statements such as A=B+C are permissible.

- DO loops are terminated by an END DO statement rather than a labeled CONTINUE. DO loops with no explicit index may be terminated by an EXIT; this is an alternative to the DO WHILE loop.

- The WHERE and CASE statements are useful new constructs.

- Subprograms are internal or external. Internal subprograms follow a CONTAINS statement and have access to all variables in the corresponding program unit. Dummy variables of subprograms may be declared to have INTENT IN, OUT, or INOUT.

- Fortran 90 has several new intrinsic functions, and also allows recursive functions. The value of a function may be an entire array.

- Formats may be defined by character variables, obviating the need for FORMAT statements.

EXERCISES 4.1

4.1.1. Combine the following Fortran 77 statements into single Fortran 90 statements.

(a) REAL PI   (b) INTEGER I(4)
    PARAMETER(PI=3.14)   DATA I/4*0/

4.1.2. Write the Fortran 90 statements that will first declare a real two-dimensional array A to be allocatable, then allocate space for A to be 50×100, and then deallocate this space.

4.1.3. Replace the following Fortran 77 loops by single Fortran 90 statements.

```
(a)     DO 1 I = 1, 10
          IF(A(I).LT.0) THEN
            A(I) = -A(I)
          END IF
     1    CONTINUE
```

(b)
```
      DO 1 I = 1,10
        DO 2 J = 1,10
          A(I,J) = B(I,J) + C(I,J)
    2   CONTINUE
    1   CONTINUE
```

4.1.4. Replace the following DO WHILE construction by a DO loop with no index and an EXIT statement.

```
K = 1
DO WHILE(A(K)<10.AND.K<=100)
    A(K) = A(K) + 1
    K=K + 1
END DO
```

4.1.5. Replace the following IF statement construction by the Fortran 90 CASE construct.

```
IF(I==1)THEN
    A(I) = 0
ELSE IF(I <= 4)THEN
    A(I)=A(I) * A(I)
ELSE
    A(I) = ABS(A(I))
END IF
```

4.1.6. Rewrite the function of Figure 3.4.1 using Fortran 90 constructs. In particular, give all dummy variables the correct INTENT.

4.1.7. Write the subroutine of Figure 3.4.2 as a Fortran 90 function.

4.1.8. Write the following output statements using a character string to define the format information.

```
        WRITE(7,10) X, Y, Z
10      FORMAT(1X, 3F8.3)
```

4.2

FORTRAN 90: ADVANCED FEATURES

Variable Kinds

Fortran 90 allows the specification of the length or precision of REAL or INTEGER variables by means of a *kind-type parameter*. For example, the statements

```
INTEGER, PARAMETER :: I8 = SELECTED_INT_KIND(8)
```
$$(4.2.1)$$
```
INTEGER(KIND = I8) :: I,J
```

specify that I and J are integers with magnitudes that can be represented by eight decimal digits; that is, magnitudes up to 99999999. Similarly, the statements

```
INTEGER,PARAMETER :: DOUB=SELECTED_REAL_KIND(14,50)
REAL(KIND = DOUB) :: A,B
```

specify that A and B are real variables with a precision of 14 decimal digits and a magnitude in the range 10^{-50} to 10^{50}. Note that this type of specification obviates the need for the DOUBLE PRECISION type, although it still exists as part of Fortran 77. In the above constructions, SELECTED_INT_KIND and SELECTED_REAL_KIND are intrinsic functions.

If the kind of a variable is not specified, it is of the *default kind*, which is defined by the particular computer system being used. For example, the default kind for integers may allow the range -32768 to 32767, corresponding to 16 bits, and the default kind for real variables may correspond to 32 bits. The advantage of the kind specification is that it allows specification of the precision needed, independent of a particular computer. The minimum precision specified will be guaranteed, although greater precision may be provided. For example, in (6.2.1) most systems would use 32 bits for I and J, giving allowable magnitudes up to approximately 2×10^9 (see Table 1.1).

Additional character kinds may also be defined to handle other character sets, such as the Greek alphabet, Japanese or Chinese symbols, and so on. Of course, the computer system being used must support such character sets. If Greek is supported and its kind is 10, then the declaration

```
CHARACTER(LEN = 50, KIND = 10) :: GREEK_WORD
```

declares GREEK_WORD to be a string variable of up to 50 Greek letters.

Derived Types

In addition to the *intrinsic data types* of REAL, INTEGER, COMPLEX, LOGICAL, and CHARACTER, Fortran 90 allows other data types, called *derived types*, to be defined. An example of this is given in Figure 4.2.1.

The statements of Figure 4.2.1 *define* the type CAR and the statement

```
TYPE(CAR) :: DODGE
```

declares DODGE to be of type CAR. The variable DODGE is called a *structure* and is composed of three *components* (WEIGHT, LENGTH, ID_NUMBER). Each of these components may be referenced separately; for example, the

```
TYPE CAR
   REAL :: WEIGHT
   REAL :: LENGTH
   INTEGER :: ID_NUMBER
END TYPE CAR
```

FIGURE 4.2.1
A derived type

first component of the structure DODGE is referenced by

DODGE%WEIGHT

It is a real variable and may be used as such in arithmetic expressions. Values may be assigned to the variable DODGE by a *structure constructor*, such as

DODGE = CAR(3250.0,184.0,12321.0)

We note that each component of a structure may itself be a structure; for example, the component WEIGHT might be a structure consisting of the weights of the engine, the transmission, and so on. We will see shortly how we can define operations on derived types.

Modules

A powerful feature of Fortran 90 is the *module*, which is useful in particular for dealing with derived data types. The usual operations (for example, $\pm, =, .$AND.) will not work with non-trivial derived data types, but we may define suitable operations by means of subprograms. We will illustrate this for the derived data type CAR of Figure 4.2.1. Suppose that we wish to define the operator .EQ. to be used with this data type. Then, if CAR1 and CAR1 are two structures of type CAR, we could write a statement like

IF(CAR1.EQ.CAR2) THEN   (4.2.2)

We may do this as illustrated by the module in Figure 4.2.2.

The logical function of Figure 4.2.2 gives a value TRUE if the weight and length of two type CAR dummy variables A and B are the same. Note that this is an example of using derived data types as subprogram arguments. The INTERFACE construction, which we will discuss later, in this case defines the operator .EQ. by means of the function COMPARE, so that statements of the form (4.2.2) may be used. The function COMPARE is put into the module following a CONTAINS statement, as illustrated in Figure 4.2.2. In general, any number of subprograms may follow the CONTAINS statement

```
MODULE CAR_OP
  TYPE CAR
    REAL :: W, L
    INTEGER :: ID
  END TYPE CAR
  INTERFACE OPERATOR(.EQ.)
    MODULE PROCEDURE COMPARE
  END INTERFACE
  CONTAINS
  FUNCTION COMPARE(A,B)
    LOGICAL COMPARE
    TYPE(CAR) :: A, B
    IF (A%W == B%W.AND.A%L == B%L)THEN
      COMPARE = .TRUE.
    ELSE
      COMPARE = .FALSE.
    END IF
  END FUNCTION COMPARE
END MODULE CAR_OP
```

FIGURE 4.2.2
A module

in a module. We note that whenever a module CONTAINS a subprogram, the END statement of that subprogram *must* include the subprogram name.

A module is essentially a collection of data specifications, interface blocks and subprograms; it is not an executable unit by itself. A module is brought into play by the USE command:

```
USE CAR_OP
```

If a program unit (main program or subprogram) contains this USE command, then the derived data type CAR, and the corresponding operator .EQ. for that data type, are available within that program unit. The USE statement within a main program also makes the module automatically available to any internal subprograms. A module cannot access itself by means of a USE statement. A call to a module subprogram must be from a statement within the module or from a statement following the USE statement for that module.

Another use of modules is to define global data. For example, the module

```
MODULE GLOBAL_DATA
  REAL, DIMENSION(100,100) :: A, B, C
END MODULE GLOBAL_DATA
```

defines A, B, and C to be 100×100 two-dimensional arrays. Any program unit that contains the statement

    USE GLOBAL_DATA

then has access to the three arrays A, B, and C. These arrays should not be redeclared within the program unit using the module. Note that a module name itself is global and may not be used as a variable name.

If the USE statement were written as

    USE GLOBAL_DATA, ONLY : A,B

then only the arrays A and B will be available and C will not be. A similar effect may be achieved by adding the statement

    PRIVATE C

to the module GLOBAL_DATA. One might wish to do this if C is being used only as an internal array in the module, and the designer of the module does not intend it to be used outside the module. The PRIVATE designation may be used not only for array names, but also for any constants, variables, types, or procedures.

Names of variables in the module may be changed if desired. For example, the statement

    USE GLOBAL_DATA, GLOBAL_A => A

will use the module with the array name A changed to GLOBAL_A within the program unit using the module. This is useful if the name A is already being used in the program in another way. Name changes may be combined with the ONLY option:

    USE GLOBAL_DATA, ONLY : B, GLOBAL_A => A.

How modules are incorporated in a program may depend on the particular compiler being used, and you should consult that compiler's manual for this information.

Overloading

The INTERFACE operator in Figure 4.2.2 defines an *overloading* or *extending* of the operator .EQ.; that is, an additional meaning is assigned to .EQ. besides the usual one for intrinsic data types.

Another example is *assignment overloading*. If CAR is the derived type of Figure 4.2.2, and CAR1 and CAR2 two variables of this type, we might wish to write the assignment statement

$$CAR1 = CAR2 \qquad\qquad (4.2.3)$$

We can do this by, again, writing a suitable subroutine, one that will assign a variable B of type CAR to a variable A of type CAR:

```
SUBROUTINE ASSIGN(A,B)
  TYPE(CAR), INTENT(OUT) :: A
  TYPE(CAR), INTENT(IN) :: B
    A%W = B%W
    A%L = B%L
    A%ID = B%ID
END SUBROUTINE ASSIGN
```

This subroutine would be added to the module of Figure 4.2.2 as would the interface block

```
INTERFACE ASSIGNMENT(=)
  MODULE PROCEDURE ASSIGN
END INTERFACE
```

Then, in any program in which the module is USEd, the assignment statement (4.2.3) has meaning. In general, the subroutine that defines an assignment must have exactly two arguments, the first having INTENT(OUT) and the second having INTENT(IN).

Although overloading can be very useful it should be used with great care since, among other things, it may make the program less understandable.

Interface Blocks and Subprograms

We now discuss some other useful features of subprograms, all of which require the use of INTERFACE blocks. First, array arguments do not need to be declared with subscript bounds within a subprogram. For example,

```
SUBROUTINE SUB(A,B)
  REAL, DIMENSION (:) :: A
  REAL, DIMENSION (:,:) :: B
```

declares A to be a one-dimensional array and B two-dimensional. When SUB is called, A and B will have the shapes of the argument arrays in the call. For example, if the subroutine is invoked by

```
CALL SUB(R,S)
```

then A and B will take on the same shapes as R and S, where R and S have been declared, for example, by

```
REAL R(10), S(10,10)
```

A and B are called *assumed-shape* arrays. Note that in Fortran 77 the first dimension of the array S must be supplied explicitly to the subprogram, but this is not necessary with assumed-shape arrays in Fortran 90.

Related to assumed-shape arrays is the idea of an *automatic* array, which is an array local to a subprogram, but whose size is unknown before the subprogram is called. For instance, in conjunction with the previous example, suppose that C is a local one-dimensional array whose size is to be the same as that of A. Then we would add to the subprogram the declaration

```
REAL, DIMENSION(SIZE(A)) :: C                    (4.2.4)
```

Here, SIZE(A) is an intrinsic function whose value is the size of A. Similarly, string lengths of dummy arguments do not need to be specified: the asterisk in the declaration in

```
SUBROUTINE CH(S)
CHARACTER(LEN = *) :: S
```

specifies that S is a string that will take on the length of the actual argument when the subprogram is called.

In the previous example, if SUB is not an internal subprogram, then the interface must be made *explicit* by an INTERFACE block in the calling program, in order to provide the compiler with sufficient information. Such an INTERFACE block is shown in Figure 4.2.3. Note that this interface block contains only the calling sequence and declarations of the external subprogram. If an automatic array also was contained in the subprogram, a declaration of the form (4.2.4) would be added to the interface block of Figure 4.2.3.

```
INTERFACE
  SUBROUTINE SUB(A,B)
    REAL, DIMENSION(:) :: A
    REAL, DIMENSION(:,:) :: B
  END SUBROUTINE SUB
END INTERFACE
```

FIGURE 4.2.3
An interface block for assumed-shape arrays

Another feature, useful when a subprogram has a large number of arguments some of which are not always needed, is the use of *optional arguments*. Consider the statements

```
SUBROUTINE S(A,B,X,Y)

REAL, OPTIONAL :: X,Y
```
(4.2.5)

Because X and Y have been declared optional, the subroutine may be called by

```
CALL S(A,B)      or      CALL S(A,B,X)
```

which would be illegal without the OPTIONAL statement. If we wished to call S with Y but not X, we would need to specify that the third argument is indeed Y and not X; this may be done, for example, by

```
CALL S(A,B,Y = 10.0)   or  CALL S(A,B,Y = Y)  (4.2.6)
```

The optional feature may be combined with an intent declaration as in

```
REAL, INTENT(IN), OPTIONAL :: X,Y
```

A construction similar to (4.2.6) may be used without the OPTIONAL feature. For example, the subroutine with heading (4.2.5) could be called by

```
CALL S(X = W, Y = 10, A = C, B = 0)
```

This illustrates *keyword-identified arguments*, in which the arguments in the CALL statement may be in any order provided the dummy argument names are present. We may also use the correct order of the arguments for some arguments, and then keywords thereafter, for example,

```
CALL S(A,B,Y= 10, X=20)
```

As soon as a keyword argument is used, all further arguments must also use keywords. Note that the type of actual and dummy arguments must always match. Also, any procedure, except an internal procedure, may be used as a procedure argument.

Again, an interface block is necessary with the above constructions if the subprogram is not internal. For example, the statements of (4.2.5) would be put in an interface block corresponding to that of Figure 4.2.3. (If only keyword-identified arguments are used, only the first line is required in the interface block.)

To summarize, an `INTERFACE` block is needed within a calling program whenever an external subprogram is called with any of the following features:

- optional or keyword-identified arguments.

- assumed-shape or assumed-size arrays.

- the external procedure uses overloaded operations, or assignment extended to other data types.

Pointers

In many problems it is necessary to extract only selected elements of an array. Suppose that we wish to put elements 1, 4, 8, 12, 15, and 20 from a one-dimensional array A into another array B. If we define an integer array P with elements 1, 4, 8, 12, 15, 20, we may achieve this by

```
DO I = 1, 6
   B(I) = A(P(I))
END DO
```

or more simply, by just B=A(P). The array P is sometimes called a *pointer array*; its elements *point* to elements of A. The use of such pointers is common in Fortran 77, but Fortran 90 allows much more general and powerful pointers.

A *pointer* is a special kind of variable that can be made to refer to other variables. The statement

$$\text{REAL, POINTER :: R} \tag{4.2.7}$$

declares that R is a real variable with the *pointer attribute*, that is, it can be used as a pointer. It can be made to point to another real variable, say T, by the statement

$$\text{REAL, TARGET :: T} \tag{4.2.8}$$

which gives T the *target attribute*, and then by the *pointer assignment*

$$\text{R => T} \tag{4.2.9}$$

R is now an *alias* of T and may be used in place of T. For example,

```
Y = R * R
```

assigns the value T*T to Y. The statement (4.2.7) does not assign storage for R. The statement (4.2.8) does assign storage for T as well as give T the target attribute. Thus, the statement (4.2.9) assigns to R the same storage location as for T.

Note that a pointer may only be assigned to a variable with the target attribute. However, pointers may also be assigned to another pointer, so as to allow pointers to pointers, and so on. For example, if T is again declared by (4.2.8) and we have the pointer declaration

```
REAL, POINTER  ::  R,Q
```

then the statement (4.2.9) followed by

$$Q \; \Rightarrow \; R \hspace{4cm} (4.2.10)$$

would also make Q an alias of T. Thus, (4.2.8) assigns a storage location to T, and (4.2.9) and (4.2.10) assign the same location to R and Q. Hence, T, R and Q all refer to the same storage location.

Arrays may also be used as pointers. For example, the statement

```
REAL, DIMENSION(:), POINTER  ::  X
```

declares X to be a pointer to a one-dimensional real array. Thus, if we have the statements

```
REAL, DIMENSION(10), TARGET  ::  B
X => B
```

then X becomes an alias for B and the statement

```
X(2) = X(2) + 1.0
```

is equivalent to B(2)=B(2) + 1.0. But X may also point to a row or column of a two-dimensional array. For example, after the statements

```
REAL, DIMENSION(100,100), TARGET  ::  A
```
$$\hspace{8cm} (4.2.11)$$
```
X => A(2,:)
```

X is an alias of the second row of A. (Consider trying to do a similar thing in Fortran 77: We could assign a row of A to a one-dimensional array X, but only by replicating the storage. X would now be a completely independent array, as opposed to an alias of a row of A.)

Two- and higher-dimensional arrays may also be pointers. For example, if

```
REAL, DIMENSION(:,:), POINTER  ::  C
```

and A is the target (4.2.11), then the assignment

```
C => A(11:20, 21:30)
```

aliases C, as a 10×10 array, with the indicated subarray of A. In this case, the indices of C run from 1 to 10, so that C(1,1) is the same as A(11,21).

As discussed above, storage for pointers is defined by assignment to a target, but storage may also be assigned directly by an ALLOCATE statement. For example,

```
ALLOCATE(R, X(-5:4))                              (4.2.12)
```

would assign storage for two of the pointers discussed above. On the other hand, a target may be defined without allocating storage, as in

```
REAL, DIMENSION(:), TARGET :: B
```

This declares that B may be the target of a pointer, but storage has not yet been assigned; it can be assigned later by an ALLOCATE statement, or by assignment to a pointer that has storage allocated. For example, if the pointer X has storage allocated by (4.2.12), the statement X => B associates that same storage with B.

A pointer will have an *unassociated* status if it is not assigned to a target; this will be the case when it is first defined. After it has been associated with a target by, for example, X => B, this association may be changed by a new assignment, for example, X => A(2,:). Or a pointer may be *disassociated* from any target by a NULLIFY statement; for example

```
NULLIFY(X)
```

disassociates X from the target to which it was previously pointing and leaves it unassociated. Moreover, if storage for X had previously been assigned by a statement such as (4.2.12), this storage is released by the NULLIFY statement. We note that trying to use unassociated pointers can lead to errors that are sometimes difficult to find.

The status of a pointer may be tested by the ASSOCIATED intrinsic function; thus,

```
ASSOCIATED(X)
```

returns a value TRUE if X is associated with a target and FALSE if not. Association with a specific target may be tested by a statement of the form

```
ASSOCIATED(X,B)
```

which returns TRUE if X points to B and FALSE otherwise.

Dummy arguments of procedures may have the pointer attribute, in which case the corresponding actual argument must also have this attribute. On the other hand, an actual argument may be a pointer even though the dummy argument is not; in this case the target of the pointer replaces the dummy argument upon invocation of the procedure. If a dummy argument is a pointer in an external procedure, there must be an interface block showing this. Moreover, if a dummy argument is a pointer, it must not be given an INTENT, nor can it be regarded as an assumed-shape array. Just as output variables of a procedure may be pointers, so may be a function value.

Pointers may also be used with derived types, for example,

```
TYPE(CAR), POINTER :: PC
```

where CAR is the data type defined in Figure 4.2.1. If DODGE is a variable of TYPE CAR, the statement

```
PC => DODGE
```

then makes PC an alias for DODGE.

Pointers and Matrices

We next consider an example of using pointers in conjunction with matrices. Suppose that A is an $N \times N$ upper triangular matrix:

$$A = \begin{bmatrix} a_{11} & \cdots & & a_{1N} \\ 0 & a_{22} & & \vdots \\ \vdots & & \ddots & \ddots \\ 0 & \cdots & 0 & a_{NN} \end{bmatrix}$$

If we store A in a two-dimensional array, then almost half the storage will consist of zeros and will be wasted if it is never used. Consequently, in many problems in scientific computing, it is customary to store only the non-zero elements of a matrix (at least only those entries that may be non-zero). For example, an upper triangular matrix could be stored in a one-dimensional array, as illustrated in Figure 4.2.4 for N=6.

The problem now is to access elements of this matrix. Since it is stored in a one-dimensional array, we cannot use the two-dimensional designation A(I,J) to access the I,J element. Instead, we must compute the location of this element in the one-dimensional array. We define an N-long, one-dimensional integer array P, whose elements will be the starting positions of each row of the matrix in the one-dimensional array, which we henceforth also denote by A. Then

$$P(1) = 1, P(2) = N+1, P(3) = 2N, P(4) = 3N-2, \ldots, P(N) = N(N+1)/2$$

$a_{11}a_{12}a_{13}a_{14}a_{15}a_{16}$	$a_{22}a_{23}a_{24}a_{25}a_{26}$	$a_{33}a_{34}a_{35}a_{36}$	$a_{44}a_{45}a_{46}$	$a_{55}a_{56}$	a_{66}
1	7	12	16	19	21

FIGURE 4.2.4
Storage for an upper triangular matrix

That is, since the first row has N elements, the second row will begin at position N+1. The second row has N-1 elements, thus the third row will begin at position N+1+N-1 = 2N, and so on. This is illustrated in Figure 4.2.4 for N=6, in which the position of the first element in each row is shown in the box below the corresponding row. In general, the integer P(I) "points" to the Ith row of the matrix so that A(P(I)) is the first element of the Ith row and A(P(I)-1+J) is the Jth element in the Ith row.

The above means of accessing elements of a triangular matrix may be carried out in Fortran 77. Next we wish to see how we can perform the analogous task using pointers in Fortran 90. It would seem natural to attempt to use an array of pointers corresponding to the array P above. Arrays of pointers are not permitted in Fortran 90, but essentially the same effect may be achieved by the use of derived types.

We first define the type ROW by

```
TYPE ROW
   REAL, DIMENSION(:), POINTER :: R     END TYPE
ROW
```

which says that variables of type ROW are pointers to one-dimensional arrays; they will point to rows of the matrix in what follows. We next declare an allocatable array of type ROW by

```
TYPE(ROW), DIMENSION(:), ALLOCATABLE :: A
```

and we allocate storage for A by

```
ALLOCATE(A(N))
```

Note that each A(I) is a structure whose only component is a pointer.

Up to this point, nothing has been done that is particular to a triangular matrix: for each I = 1, ..., N, A(I)%R is just a pointer to a one-dimensional array. We next allocate storage for these pointers in a way that is compatible with a triangular matrix:

```
DO I = 1, N
   ALLOCATE(A(I)%R(I:N))
END DO
```

Now, the pointer A(I)%R has been allocated storage for a one-dimensional array with indices I, I+1, ..., N, just what is needed for the Ith row of an upper triangular matrix. The I, J element in this matrix may be accessed by A(I)%R(J). For example, the following statements will assign the value

```
DO I = 1, N
   B(I) = 0
   DO J = I, N
      B(I) = B(I) + A(I)%R(J)*X(J)
   END DO
END DO
```

FIGURE 4.2.5
Triangular matrix-vector multiplication

I+J to the I, J element:

```
DO I = 1, N
 DO J = I, N
  A(I)%R(J) = I+J
 END DO
END DO
```

As another example, the code segment in Figure 4.2.5 will compute the product of the triangular matrix A and a vector X, putting the result vector into the array B. We assume that X and B have been declared as N-long, one-dimensional arrays.

We note that if A had been declared as a two-dimensional array, the code for triangular matrix-vector multiplication would be identical to that of Figure 4.2.5, with the exception that the arithmetic statement would be replaced by

```
B(I) = A(I,J)*X(J)
```

MAIN POINTS OF SECTION 4.2

- The (minimum) precision of real or integer variables may be specified by a kind-type parameter. This obviates the need for the double precision type.

- Derived types may be defined by the programmer. Operations on derived types and overloading of operators may be defined by means of subprograms and interface blocks.

- Modules provide a mechanism for sharing data, subprograms, derived types, and new operators across different program units. Modules are brought into play by the USE statement.

- Arrays in subprograms may be assumed-shape or automatic. Subprogram arguments may be optional or keyword-identified. Interface blocks are required for external subprograms in all these cases.

- Pointers provide a mechanism for aliasing variables, including arrays and array sections.

EXERCISES 4.2

4.2.1. Write the declaration statements that define I to be an integer variable with allowable magnitude of at least six decimal digits, and A a real variable with magnitude in the range 10^{-30} to 10^{30} and precision of at least 10 decimal digits.

4.2.2. Define a derived type PLANE with three components: the weights of the wings, fuselage, and remainder of aircraft. Then write one or more statements that will assign values to the three components.

4.2.3. Modify Figure 4.2.2 so as to pertain to the derived type of Exercise 4.2.2. Define also an overloading of assignment for this data type.

4.2.4. Write a subroutine with the dummy variables A, B, C, I, where A is a two-dimensional array, B is a one-dimensional array, C is real, and I is integer. Allow for A and B to be assumed-shape arrays and define a local automatic array, D, that will take on the size of B. Allow also for all dummy variables to be optional or keyword-identified. Write the INTERFACE block to go with the above specifications.

4.2.5. Modify the statements given in the text for using pointers to access an upper-triangular matrix so that they apply to a lower-triangular matrix.

4.3

OBSOLESCENT FEATURES

Fortran 77 has several features that have been considered obsolete for many years and, by and large, are no longer used in writing new programs. Although they are officially part of Fortran 90, since all of Fortran 77 is, at least some of these obsolescent features may well be deleted from future Fortran standards. However, they might appear in older programs, and in order to read and/or modify such programs it is necessary to understand them. These are described first, then more current features of Fortran 77 that are obsolescent by virtue of Fortran 90 are described. Again, these features should be avoided in writing new programs, but their use will be pervasive in existing programs for some years to come. Moreover, in modifying an existing program it may well be more practical to use Fortran 77 constructs, rather than attempting to mix in Fortran 90 features.

Older Obsolete Features

We now discuss a few Fortran 77 features that were considered obsolete even before the introduction of Fortran 90. These are features that should not be used in writing new programs, but might appear in very old programs.

DIMENSION Statement

In the original Fortran, arrays were declared by statements of the form

    DIMENSION A(10,10)   (4.3.1)

In Fortran 77 this was superseded by the use of a type declaration:

    REAL A(10,10)   (4.3.2)

It is interesting that their combination is the preferred style in Fortran 90:

    REAL, DIMENSION(10,10) :: A

Computed GO TO

The statement

    GO TO (10,20,30) I   (4.3.3)

transfers control to statement 10 if $I=1$, to statement 20 if $I=2$, to statement 30 if $I=3$, and no transfer occurs if I is any other value. The variable I in (4.3.3) may be replaced by an expression; for example,

    GO TO (200,100) I - J + 1

will transfer to statement 200 if $I - J +1$ is 1, statement 100 if $I - J+1$ is 2, and no transfer otherwise.

Assigned GO TO

In the assigned GO TO statement, a statement number is first assigned to an integer variable, for example,

    ASSIGN 10 TO I

Then when the statement

    GO TO I   (4.3.4)

is encountered, I is replaced by its current assigned value. One use of this construction was to set branches to different locations, depending on some condition. For example, the IF statement

```
IF(N.EQ.0) THEN
    ASSIGN 10 TO I
ELSE
    ASSIGN 20 TO I
END IF
```

would set the transfer (4.3.4), depending on the value of N.

Arithmetic IF

Somewhat related to the computed and assigned GO TO statements is the arithmetic IF statement. For example,

```
IF(I) 10, 20, 30
```

will transfer control to statement 10 if I<0, to statement 20 if I=0, and to statement 30 if I>0.

Features Obsolete Because of Fortran 90

We have already mentioned several Fortran 77 features that have been superseded by Fortran 90. We first will briefly summarize these, and then consider other features not yet discussed.

Fixed-form source code, that is, statements in columns 7–72 and so on, is replaced by free-form source code. Recall that the two forms cannot be mixed in the same program unit.

Statement functions may be replaced by internal functions. More generally, internal subprograms may be either functions or subroutines.

The DATA statement will usually be replaced by assignment of values in the declaration statement, although in certain cases, such as initializing all values of a large array, the DATA statement may still be useful.

The DOUBLE PRECISION data type is replaced by a suitable KIND declaration.

The CONTINUE statement terminating a DO loop is replaced by an END DO statement, and a statement label is no longer used. The DO LOOP may also be given a name.

The DO WHILE construct (or WHILE DO on some Fortran 77 systems) may be replaced by a DO loop with an IF ( ) EXIT statement for termination.

FORMAT statements may be replaced by assignment of edit descriptors to character variables.

Note that with the changes in the DO statement and FORMAT statement, statement labels are no longer necessary except in those rare instances when a GO TO statement must be used.

There are various possible forms of the CHARACTER declaration statement, for example, CHARACTER*10, A, B, C*2, and several other equivalent declarations not discussed in the text. Character strings may now be declared using the form

```
CHARACTER(LEN = 10)  ::  A,B
```

We next discuss some other Fortran 77 features that have not previously been mentioned.

EQUIVALENCE

If A and B are two real variables, the statement

```
EQUIVALENCE(A,B)
```
(4.3.5)

assigns both A and B to the same memory location. Similarly, other intrinsic data types such as integers may be made equivalent, as well as arrays of the same shape; for example, if A and B were each 100×100 real arrays, the statement (4.3.5) would assign both arrays to the same storage.

One original motivation for the EQUIVALENCE statement was to conserve storage, but still allow different variable names in different parts of a program. For example, suppose that in the first part of a program the array A is needed, but after a certain point it is no longer required. Rather than using new storage for a second array B, needed only in the latter part of the program, the space reserved for A could be reused. The EQUIVALENCE statement in this context may be replaced in Fortran 90 by dynamic storage allocation using allocatable arrays, or by pointers.

IMPLICIT Declarations

As discussed previously, variables that are not explicitly declared are implicitly assumed to be INTEGER if the first letter is I, J, K, L, M, N, and REAL otherwise. Fortran 77 allows this convention to be modified by statements such as

```
IMPLICIT INTEGER(A,B)
IMPLICIT REAL(C - Z)
```

Then, any variable beginning with A or B is integer and the rest are real, if not otherwise declared. This is not recommended, however. As already discussed, it is always best to use the Fortran 90 feature

```
IMPLICIT NONE
```

This then forces all variables to be declared, or a compile-time error will occur.

ENTRY

Fortran 77 allows subprograms to be entered in more than one place by means of the ENTRY statement. For example, in the function

```
FUNCTION F(X)
   statements
ENTRY G(X)
   statements
END FUNCTION F
```

a call in the main program of the form Y=G(X) will enter the function at the point of the ENTRY statement. This is sometimes useful when two different functions are almost identical, and most of the code can be utilized for both. The ENTRY statement is made unnecessary by the use of modules.

COMMON Storage

Global variables that are available to both the main program and subprograms may be accomplished in Fortran 77 by the COMMON statement. This statement has been made obsolete by modules in Fortran 90. Nevertheless, the COMMON statement has been in wide use, and an understanding of its basic properties may be necessary to read many existing large programs. Therefore, we will describe it in some detail. Figure 4.3.1 gives an example of the use of COMMON statements.

In Figure 4.3.1, the first COMMON statement sets aside storage for B, C, M, N in the main program, and the second COMMON statement assigns exactly the same storage to the variables R, S, I, J in the subroutine. This is illustrated in Figure 4.3.2, in which B and R refer to the same storage location, and so on.

Suppose that in the main program, B has the value 3.12 when the subroutine is called. Then in the subroutine the variable R has this exact same value since B and R refer to the same storage location. Note that the variable names in the main program and subprograms referring to this COMMON storage may be different, but *they must always be the same type*. In particular, we cannot associate real and integer variables, since they may require different amounts of storage. Moreover, variables appearing in COMMON

```
PROGRAM EXAM
REAL B,C
INTEGER M,N
COMMON B,C,M,N
   .
   .
   .

SUBROUTINE SUB(X,Y,Z)
REAL R,S,X,Y,Z
INTEGER I,J
COMMON R,S,I,J
   .
   .
   .
```

FIGURE 4.3.1
COMMON statements

Main Program	B	R	Subroutine
	C	S	
	M	I	
	N	J	

FIGURE 4.3.2
COMMON storage

statements of a subprogram may not be used as formal arguments in that subprogram. For example, the statements

```
SUBROUTINE S(X,Y)
   REAL X,Y
   COMMON Y
```

are not permitted.

As a second example, suppose that there is also a function that is called by the main program or subroutine of Figure 4.3.1, and this function has the statements shown in Figure 4.3.3. The variable Y in this function is associated with the variables B and R in common storage and will use this value when the arithmetic statement in Figure 4.3.3 is executed. Note that in this case the function uses only one of the four storage locations in the common area.

The association of variables in common storage is solely positional: the first variable in the COMMON statement associates with the first storage

```
FUNCTION F(X)
   REAL F, X, Y
   COMMON Y
   F = X * X + Y
END
```

FIGURE 4.3.3
A function using COMMON
storage

position, the second variable with the second position, and so on. If in Figure 4.3.3 you wished Y to be associated with the variable C in the main program, rather than B, then you must change the COMMON statement in Figure 4.3.3 to, say,

```
COMMON Z,Y
```

where Z is just an extra variable that is not used in the function.

Arrays may also be associated in common storage, even when they are not the same size. For example, Figure 4.3.4 shows an array of length 6 in the main program and an array of length 8 in a subroutine, both assigned to common storage. Here, A(I) and B(I) occupy the same storage locations for I = 1, ..., 6, but the locations for B(7) and B(8) have no counterparts in A.

Figure 4.3.4 also illustrates common storage of one-dimensional and two-dimensional arrays. Extreme caution must be used in this type of as-

```
PROGRAM QR
REAL A(6)
COMMON A
   .
   .
   .
SUBROUTINE S(X,Y)
   REAL B(8), X,Y
   COMMON B
   .
   .
   .
FUNCTION F(Z)
   REAL F, Z, D(3,3)
   COMMON  D
```

FIGURE 4.3.4
COMMON statements for arrays

$$
\begin{array}{lll}
A(1) \longleftrightarrow B(1) \longleftrightarrow D(1,1) \\
A(2) \longleftrightarrow B(2) \longleftrightarrow D(2,1) \\
A(3) \longleftrightarrow B(3) \longleftrightarrow D(3,1) \\
A(4) \longleftrightarrow B(4) \longleftrightarrow D(1,2) \\
A(5) \longleftrightarrow B(5) \longleftrightarrow D(2,2) \\
A(6) \longleftrightarrow B(6) \longleftrightarrow D(3,2) \\
 B(7) \longleftrightarrow D(1,3) \\
 B(8) \longleftrightarrow D(2,3) \\
 D(3,3)
\end{array}
$$

FIGURE 4.3.5
COMMON storage for Figure 4.3.4

sociation, keeping in mind that elements of two-dimensional arrays will be stored in column-major order. The storage association for the example of Figure 4.3.4 is shown in Figure 4.3.5. Generally, it is good practice to match only arrays of the same shapes in common storage.

Additional common storage areas may be defined by assigning them names. For example, the COMMON statements in Figure 4.3.4 could be written as

```
COMMON/RC/A
COMMON/RC/B
COMMON/RC/D
```

In this case, an area of common storage named RC is set aside. If no name is used, as in the previous examples, the storage area is called *blank* common and may also be denoted by COMMON//A. Both blank common and named common areas may be declared in the same program, and each refers to a different storage area. But there are two important differences between named and blank common. First, at the termination of a subprogram, data in a named common block may become undefined, although it remains defined with blank common. Secondly, named common blocks with the same name must be the same size in all programs/subprograms that use them; this is not necessary for blank common.

Common storage is replaced in Fortran 90 by the use of modules. For example, as discussed in Section 4.2, the module

```
MODULE GLOBAL_DATA
   REAL, DIMENSION(100,100) :: A,B,C
END MODULE GLOBAL_DATA
```

declares three arrays that may be used in the main program and any subprogram by the statement

```
USE GLOBAL_DATA
```

BLOCK DATA

The DATA statement may not ordinarily be used to initialize variables assigned to common storage. However, it may be used for this purpose to initialize variables in a named common block (but not blank common) by means of a BLOCK DATA program. The following is an example.

```
BLOCK DATA
  REAL A(10,10), B(10), C(10)
  COMMON/MAIN/A, B, C
  DATA A/100*0/
  DATA B/10*1.0/
  DATA C/10*2.0/
END
```

The END statement signifies that this is a separate program unit that would usually be placed at the beginning of the main program or subprogram. It assigns the three arrays A, B, and C to a COMMON block named MAIN, then initializes them.

Since the BLOCK DATA construct is used only with common storage, it also becomes obsolete in Fortran 90.

MAIN POINTS OF SECTION 4.3

- Some older Fortran 77 features that have been obsolete for some time are the computed GO TO, the assigned GO TO, and the arithmetic IF.

- Some Fortran features that become of lesser importance in Fortran 90 are: the DATA statement, statement functions, and FORMAT statements.

- The DO WHILE construction is part of Fortran 90, but the IF ( )EXIT in a DO loop with no index is an attractive alternative.

- Some Fortran 77 features that are obsolete because of Fortran 90 are: Fixed-form source code, the double precision data type, the CONTINUE statement terminating DO loops, the EQUIVALENCE statement, IMPLICIT declarations, and the ENTRY statement.

- Common storage is replaced by the use of modules, and the BLOCK DATA construction for initializing data in named common blocks becomes obsolete.

CAVEATS
AND FURTHER
READING

This book is meant to be only an introduction and not a definitive coverage of the Fortran language. Although we have treated most features of Fortran 77 completely, we have covered only the basic parts of input/output. Further details on Fortran 77 may be obtained from the reference manual for the system you are using or from a number of books. A few references are:

Edgar, S., *Fortran for the 90's*. New York: Computer Science Press, 1992.

Etter, D. M., *Structured Fortran 77 for Scientists and Engineers*. 4th ed., Redwood City, CA: Benjamin/Cummings Publishing Co., 1993.

Nyhoff, L., and S. Leestma. *Fortran 77 for Engineers and Scientists*. 3rd ed., New York: MacMillan Publishing Co., 1992.

These references also include numerous applications from science and engineering. Additional references for Fortran 90 are:

Brainerd, W., C. Goldberg, J. Adams. *Programmer's Guide to Fortran 90*. New York: McGraw-Hill, 1990.

Metcalf, M. and J. Reid. *Fortran 90 Explained*. New York: Oxford University Press, 1990.

The book by Brainard et al. gives a number of examples of Fortran 90 programs, including the interesting topic of using pointers to construct linked lists.

     Our introduction to numerical methods for scientific computing has necessarily been at an elementary level, and some of the methods discussed are not the best for most applications. This is especially true of the methods for numerical integration and for differential equations. More advanced discussions of these topics are given in a number of books devoted to numerical methods; two references are:

Burden, R. and J. D. Faires. *Numerical Analysis.* 4th ed., Boston: PWS-Kent Publishing Company, 1989.

Golub, G. and J. Ortega. *Scientific Computing and Differential Equations.* New York: Academic Press, 1992.

Although our treatment of Gaussian elimination is reasonably complete, at least at this level, the reader is advised to use the subroutines in LAPACK, if it is available. LAPACK replaces LINPACK, which has been the standard package of linear equation solvers for over a decade. A reference is:

Anderson, E., Z. Bai, C. Bischof, J. Demmel, J. Dongarra, J. DuCroz, A. Greenbaum, S. Hammarling, A. McKenney, S. Ostrouchov, and D. Sorensen. *LAPACK User's Guide.* Philadelphia: SIAM, 1992.

ASCII CHARACTER CODES

Character	Binary (Decimal)	Character	Binary (Decimal)	Character	Binary (Decimal)
A	1000001 (65)	a	1100001 (97)	0	0110000 (48)
B	1000010 (66)	b	1100010 (98)	1	0110001 (49)
C	1000011 (67)	c	1100011 (99)	2	0110010 (50)
D	1000100 (68)	d	1100100 (100)	3	0110011 (51)
E	1000101 (69)	e	1100101 (101)	4	0110100 (52)
F	1000110 (70)	f	1100110 (102)	5	0110101 (53)
G	1000111 (71)	g	1100111 (103)	6	0110110 (54)
H	1001000 (72)	h	1101000 (104)	7	0110111 (55)
I	1001001 (73)	i	1101001 (105)	8	0111000 (56)
J	1001010 (74)	j	1101010 (106)	9	0111001 (57)
K	1001011 (75)	k	1101011 (107)		0100000 (32)
L	1001100 (76)	l	1101100 (108)	!	0100001 (33)
M	1001101 (77)	m	1101101 (109)	"	0100010 (34)
N	1001110 (78)	n	1101110 (110)	#	0100011 (35)
O	1001111 (79)	o	1101111 (111)	$	0100100 (36)
P	1010000 (80)	p	1110000 (112)	%	0100101 (37)
Q	1010001 (81)	q	1110001 (113)	&	0100110 (38)
R	1010010 (82)	r	1110010 (114)	'	0100111 (39)
S	1010011 (83)	s	1110011 (115)	(	0101000 (40)
T	1010100 (84)	t	1110100 (116)	)	0101001 (41)
U	1010101 (85)	u	1110101 (117)	*	0101010 (42)
V	1010110 (86)	v	1110110 (118)	+	0101011 (43)
W	1010111 (87)	w	1110111 (119)	,	0101100 (44)
X	1011000 (88)	x	1111000 (120)	-	0101101 (45)
Y	1011001 (89)	y	1111001 (121)	.	0101110 (46)
Z	1011010 (90)	z	1111010 (122)	/	0101111 (47)
[	1011011 (91)	{	1111011 (123)	:	0111010 (58)
\	1011100 (92)			1111100 (124)	;	0111011 (59)
]	1011101 (93)	}	1111101 (125)	<	0111100 (60)
∧	1011110 (94)			=	0111101 (61)
_	1011111 (95)			>	0111110 (62)
'	1100000 (96)			?	0111111 (63)
				@	0100000 (64)

INTRINSIC
FUNCTIONS

An intrinsic function is *generic* if it can accept arguments of different types and return a value appropriate for the type of argument. For example, the function ABS is generic and may be used with integer, real, double precision, and complex arguments. In each case, it returns the absolute value appropriate for the argument: integer for integer, real for real or complex, double precision for double precision. In addition to the generic name, many functions also have specific names depending on the argument; for example, IABS, ABS, DABS, and CABS are the specific names corresponding to integer, real, double precision and complex arguments. Specific names *must* be used when the function is an argument of a subprogram. In the following, we give the generic name of the function first, followed by specific names, if any. In many cases, the generic name is also specific for the most common argument, usually real.

Mathematical Functions

In all the mathematical functions, the argument is real, double precision, or complex.

SQRT(X) is generic. X must be nonnegative if real or double. It can also be complex, including negative real numbers. DSQRT, CSQRT are specific.

EXP(X) is generic. DEXP and CEXP are specific.

LOG(X), LOG10(X) are generic. LOG10 gives base 10 log. ALOG and ALOG10 specific for real, DLOG and DLOG10 specific for double, CLOG for complex. No specific name for complex LOG10.

SIN(X), COS(X), TAN(X) are generic. Arguments are in radians. DSIN, CSIN, DCOS, CCOS, DTAN are specific. No specific name for complex TAN.

ASIN(X), ACOS(X), ATAN(X), ATAN2(X, Y) are generic. ATAN2(X, Y) gives arctangent of X/Y. Results are in radians. DASIN, DACOS, DATAN, DATANZ are specific. No complex specific.

SINH(X), COSH(X) are generic. DSINH, DCOSH are specific. No complex specific.

Maximum and Minimum Functions

Arguments for these functions are integer, real, or double.

MAX(X, Y, ...) is generic. Gives maximum of any number of arguments. For integer arguments, MAX0 and AMAX0 are specific and give integer and real results, respectively. For real arguments, MAX1 and AMAX1 are specific and give integer and real results, respectively. DMAX specific for double.

MIN(X, Y, ...) is generic. MIN0, AMIN0, MIN1, AMIN1, DMIN analogous to those for MAX.

DIM(X, Y) is generic. Gives $\max(X - Y, 0)$. IDIM and DDIM specific.

Number Conversion Functions

ABS(X) is generic. Gives absolute value for integer, real, complex, and double. IABS, ABS, CABS, DABS are specific.

REAL(X) is generic. Converts integer to real. FLOAT is specific.

SNG(X) converts double to single precision.

INT(X) is generic. Truncates real or double to integer. IFIX is specific for real. IDINT is specific for double.

NINT(X) is generic. Rounds real or double to nearest integer. IDNINT specific for double.

AINT(X) is generic. Rounds real or double to nearest integer, but function value is real (or double). DINT specific for double.

SIGN(X,Y) is generic. Gives $|X|$ if $Y \geq 0$ and $-|X|$ otherwise. ISIGN and DSIGN specific for integer and double.

MOD(X,Y) is generic. Gives remainder of X/Y. AMOD and DMOD specific for real and double.

DBLE(X) is generic. Converts real or integer to double. No specific names.

CMPLX(X) is generic. Converts real, integer or double to complex. No specific names.

DPROD(X,Y) is specific. Gives double precision product of two reals.

REAL(X) gives real part of complex number.

AIMAG(X) gives imaginary part of complex number.

CONJG(X) gives complex conjugate of complex number.

Character Manipulation Functions

The following functions are all specific.

INDEX(C1,C2) gives position of first occurence of string C2 in string C1, or 0 if no occurence.

LEN(C) gives length of string C.

CHAR(I) gives character in the Ith position in the ASCII collating sequence.

ICHAR(C) gives position of the character C in the ASCII collating sequence.

LGE(C1,C2) gives TRUE if C1 is lexically greater than or equal to C2. FALSE otherwise.

LGT, LLT, LLE similar to LGE with comparison on greater than, less than, and less than or equal to.

Selected Fortran 90 Intrinsic Functions

All Fortran 77 intrinsic functions are part of Fortran 90. There are several additional Fortran 90 functions and the following is just a sampling. Moreover, many of these functions have optional parameters that are not given here.

Mathematical Functions

CEILING (X). Least integer $\geq X$.

FLOOR (X). Greatest integer $\leq X$.

DOT_PRODUCT (A, B). Dot product of vectors A and B.

MATMUL (A, B). Product of matrices A and B.

MAXVAL (A). Maximum value of elements of real or integer array A.

MINVAL (A). Minimum value of elements of real or integer array A.

MAXLOC (A). Location of maximum element in array A.

MINLOC (A). Location of minimum element in array A.

PRODUCT (A). Product of elements of array A.

SUM (A). Sum of elements of array A.

TRANSPOSE (A). Transpose of two-dimensional array A.

Number Manipulation Functions

EXPONENT (X). Exponent part of X.

FRACTION (X). Mantissa of X.

ISHFT (I, S). Shifts an integer I to the left S bits.

SELECTED_INT_KIND (I). Kind of type parameter.

SELECTED_REAL_KIND (I, J). Kind of type parameter.

SIZE (A). Number of elements in the array A.

Logical Functions

ALL (L). True if all elements of logical array L are true.

ANY (L). True if any element of logical array L is true.

COUNT (L). Number of true elements in logical array L.

ALLOCATED (A). True if array A is allocated.

ASSOCIATED (P). True if pointer P is associated.

BTEST (I, J). True if bit I of integer J is 1.

IAND (I, J). Logical AND of bits in I and J.

IOR(I,J). Logical OR of bits in I and J.

NOT(I). Logical complement of bits in I.

Character Functions

ADJUSTL(C). Shifts string C left to remove leading blanks.

ADJUSTR(C). Shifts string C right to remove trailing blanks.

REPEAT(C,N). Concatenates N copies of string C.

SCAN(C,S). Position of left-most character of string C that is in string S.

VERIFY(C,S). Position of left-most character of string C not in string S.

TRIM(C). Remove trailing blanks from string C.

INDEX